Violence in Our Lives

VIOLENCE IN OUR LIVES

Impact on Workplace, Home, and Community

Elizabeth K. Carll, Ph.D.

Allyn and Bacon

Boston • London • Toronto • Sydney • Tokyo • Singapore

Vice President and Editor-in-Chief, Social Sciences and Education: Sean Wakely
Editorial Assistant: Susan Hutchinson
Marketing Manager: Stephen Smith
Editorial–Production Administrator: Donna Simons
Editorial–Production Service: Matrix Productions Inc.
Composition and Prepress Buyer: Linda Cox
Manufacturing Buyer: Suzanne Lareau
Cover Administrator: Jenny Hart
Electronic Composition: Cabot Computer Services

0297548885

Library of Congress Cataloging-in-Publication Data

Carll, Elizabeth K.
    Violence in our lives : Impact on workplace, home, and community /
Elizabeth K. Carll
        p.   cm.
    Includes bibliographical references and index.
    ISBN 0-205-17085-4
    1. Violence—United States.   2. Violence in the workplace—United
States.   3. Family violence—United States.   I. Carll, Elizabeth K.
HN90.V5V5486   1998
303.6'0973—dc21   98-29111
                                                                        CIP

Cartoon on page 169 used with permission of the *New York Daily News.*
Discussion of the Radtke case, and of Justice David Goldstein as presiding
judge, on pages 180–181 used by permission of Justice Goldstein.

Printed in the United States of America
10 9 8 7 6 5 4 3 2 1   03 02 01 00 99 98

WZ MAR - - 2000

CONTENTS

ABOUT THE AUTHOR

Elizabeth K. Carll, Ph.D., is a psychologist with interests in stress and posttraumatic stress management; interpersonal, family, and workplace violence; and stress and health issues. She is a nationally recognized trauma expert and a fellow and diplomate of the American Board of Medical Psychotherapy. She has intervened and consulted in the aftermath of violence and trauma at all levels, from individual to corporate incidents to large-scale disasters. The originator of the term *trauma psychology,* she has authored more than fifty publications and papers and is in private practice in Centerport and Huntington, New York.

An advocate of community service, Dr. Carll is the founder and chair of the New York State Psychological Association (NYSPA) Disaster/ Crisis Response Network and the northeast representative of the National Advisory Committee of the American Psychological Association (APA) to the Disaster Response Network. She is also the founder and co-chair of the NYSPA Task Force on Violence and serves on the boards of a variety of community organizations. As a longtime advocate of community education, she has frequently appeared in the news media discussing psychology and issues of public interest.

ABOUT THE
CHAPTER CONTRIBUTORS

David Batza, senior vice president of Gavin de Becker Inc., has directly supervised the management of thousands of cases involving inappropriate pursuit, workplace violence, and stalking. He has designed workplace violence prevention programs for Fortune 500 companies, government agencies, and universities and is a lead designer of the computer-assisted threat assessment program called MOSAIC. Mr. Batza has prepared testimony for the California State Senate Assembly Hearing and Judiciary Committees. He is also a volunteer at domestic violence shelters, helps provide the funding for the Domestic Violence Safety Plan Hotline, and is a founding member of the Association of Threat Assessment Professionals.

Charles Patrick Ewing, J.D., Ph.D., is professor of law and adjunct professor of psychology. He received his Ph.D. from Cornell University in 1975, was a postdoctoral fellow at Yale University, and graduated with honors from Harvard Law School in 1983. He is the author or co-author of six books and is senior editor of the journal *Behavioral Sciences and the Law*. Dr. Ewing is a fellow of the American Psychological Association and a diplomate in forensic psychology of the American Board of Professional Psychology. He received the 1993 Distinguished Contributions to Forensic Psychology Award, which is presented annually by the American Academy of Forensic Psychology.

Stuart Kleinman, M.D., is a psychiatrist certified in forensic psychiatry and traumatology who has examined thousands of criminal defendants regarding such issues as "insanity" and civil litigants regarding issues of harassment and discrimination at the workplace, and who has consulted with corporations concerning workplace violence. Dr. Kleinman also has studied victims of Middle Eastern terrorism and Asian piracy and is a former medical director of a clinic that treats the psychological injuries suffered by crime victims. Currently, he maintains a private consultative and treatment practice in Manhattan, teaches at the Columbia University College of Physicians and Surgeons, and is chairman of the Committee on Victimology of the American Academy of Psychiatry and the Law.

Frederick J. Lanceley retired from the Federal Bureau of Investigation after twenty-six years of government service. During his many years assigned to the FBI Academy, his responsibilities included operations, instruction, and research. Mr. Lanceley became the FBI's senior negotiator and principal developer of its internationally recognized crisis negotiation training course. His insights, breadth of experience, and innovative instructional methods have contributed to his recognition as an international authority on crisis negotiation. He continues to train and consult on a national and international basis.

Michelle Taylor, director of threat assessment and management of Gavin de Becker Inc., has personally assessed and managed several thousand cases involving public figures and interpersonal stalking and disgruntled current and former employees. She is currently completing a master's degree in forensic sciences at National University. Ms. Taylor is often interviewed as a stalking expert and has appeared on national news programs and in magazines. She is a consultant to corporations, entertainment companies, public figures, and the criminal justice community regarding stalking, workplace violence, and public figure safety.

ACKNOWLEDGMENTS

This book would not have been possible without the support of several people. A book discussing so many different facets of violence could not have been developed without the comments of both my colleagues and my patients, who have experienced violence firsthand, all of whom provided much food for thought over the years.

Dr. Virginia Upton, psychologist, Glen Head, New York, and Dr. Catherine L. Waltz, executive director, The Peace Project, Inc., Fort Lauderdale, Florida, provided valuable suggestions and comments that helped shape the final draft. Chapter contributions from Dr. Charles Patrick Ewing, David Batza and Michelle Taylor, Frederick Lanceley, and Dr. Stuart Kleinman added breadth to the book by providing expert insights into specialized areas of violence.

Mylan Jaixan, former editor at Allyn and Bacon, supported the time-consuming evolution of the project. Carla Daves, editor at Allyn and Bacon, assumed the project and provided a smooth transition to publication. Sue Hutchinson's practical advice and comments as editorial assistant helped me navigate through the various phases to the completion of the manuscript.

Most of all, I am indebted to my husband, Alan Carll, whose patience, generosity, and pragmatic advice served as a constant source of support.

Violence in Our Lives

1

INTRODUCTION

ELIZABETH K. CARLL, Ph.D.

It is 10:00 P.M. TV sets across the country switch to local news broadcasts. Except for the few days when an extraordinary event occurs (an earthquake, a stock market crash, a major international agreement), the opening news segment remains remarkably uniform throughout the nation. A remote unit broadcasts in front of a suburban home, city apartment house, school, or business office. The area is cordoned off with police crime scene tape. An ambulance waits to take a wounded person (or persons) to the hospital—or a corpse to the morgue. The newscaster solemnly intones the known data about this latest act of violence: a family dispute, a problem over drugs, a coworker gone berserk, a gang clash at school. You know them already; you have heard them hundreds of times before on the nightly news.

This repeated exposure to scenes of violence has fostered over the years two opposite but extremely destructive attitudes in the public. On the one hand, people cannot help but feel that their society is wildly out of control and that violence reigns—at home, school, work, everywhere. Little can be done except to beef up the police and arm the citizenry or stay in one's own neighborhood and regard everyone with suspicion—in short, to develop a bunker mentality.

1

On the other hand, the scenes are so familiar and so customary that much of the public has grown inured to the terrible tragedies that occur daily. With continual incidents of violence, only the most gruesome or bizarre receive much coverage in the news. The viewing public is so sated with violence that it simply cannot respond to the loss and grief that inevitably attend such acts.

This book does *not* accept either of these attitudes, and it was written to counter both. No, the country has *not* been taken over by a race of violent extraterrestrials. It is our children, our neighbors, and ourselves who are committing violence, and it is we, as individuals, parents, workers, and members of the community, who must work to control this culture of violence. It is a difficult but not impossible task.

To that end, this book presents many real-life incidents involving violence. It takes this approach to stress that these are tragedies of real people, not cardboard cutouts or fictionalized characters in the latest movie of the week. Moreover, it offers a number of possible strategies and interventions (for both professionals and the general public) aimed at detecting and heading off possible violent incidents, as well as at alleviating the effects of trauma when they do occur. The suggestions are based on the latest research, and they cover a variety of situations: violence and terrorism in the workplace; domestic and family violence; even the effects on the public (adults and children) of continued portrayals of violence in the news, in films, and on TV. In all instances, the book works to alert readers to potentially dangerous situations and to set forth practical methods of coping with them. For this reasoned approach to an emotion-laden problem, the book will prove invaluable to all readers, health professionals, law enforcement personnel, the judiciary, the media, and the general public.

It is, however, in the area of the public's all too facile acceptance of the level of violence in our society that the book makes its major contribution. Its main goal is to persuade us, the general public, to change the way we think about violence. For instance, when a young teenager assails and kills one of his schoolmates, two young lives are destroyed—two hopes blasted—

to say nothing of the grief visited on both families. Using violence to deal with anger or frustration seems utterly natural to American society today, but the consequences of it are too often passed over. If the public were more exposed to the awful tasks of dealing with the aftermath of acts of violence and the far reaching impact on the future of society, it might be much less accepting of it as a medium of problem solving.

The purpose of this book is not only to help readers think about how devastating violence can be but also to discuss what domestic violence means for the health of families and, especially, children. Children brought up in a climate that accepts violence as a normal response to stress will use violence themselves as adults when they face frustration—and a terrible cycle is born. The book examines the many interrelated facets of violence and how to break the cycle. It means to sensitize readers to the amount of violence they are subjected to in the various media and, most especially, to expose the unspoken assumptions and prejudices that underlie the way violence is portrayed and understood in our society. The inequitable treatment of women, whether as victims or perpetrators of violence, fostered by these prejudices must be rectified.

Our society knows too much about violence now; it has seen too much of it. Familiarity has bred contempt, even indifference. I hope this book will open the reader's mind to new ways of looking at violence. The culture of violence represented in the media every day is not inevitable.

2

WORKPLACE AND COMMUNITY VIOLENCE

Intervention and Prevention

ELIZABETH K. CARLL, Ph.D.

Violence today is not confined to "bad areas." It touches all communities, even those whose inhabitants assume, "That sort of thing does not happen here." For instance, even though incidents such as the World Trade Center and Oklahoma City bombings occurred in the workplace, they were so extensive that the entire community, and even the entire country, felt their impact. Moreover, shootings in post offices, restaurants, fast-food shops, and schools are recounted in the media almost daily.

Even more troubling is the distinctly random and "impersonal" nature of many violent incidents. In a way, we can grasp an act of violence in the workplace that appears to be related to a specific issue, such as a disgruntled or terminated employee who returns to open fire on his boss or an angry husband who confronts his wife at work in a fit of jealous rage. It is not acceptable, of course, but it is comprehensible. What, however, can we make of what seems to be totally gratuitous violence? A person suddenly attacks people he does not know and who are in no way involved with him. It certainly was not anything they did personally, so how can they even imagine how to protect themselves from such an incident? The terror such acts arouse in a community stems largely from the sense of helplessness they create.

My own sense of personal security about living in a neighborhood that was long considered safe from random violence was shattered as I drove to the hospital the evening of the Long Island Railroad shootings, an incident that gained nationwide attention in the media. I had just concluded a session with my last patient when I received an emergency call from the American Red Cross to assist family members of the shooting victims, arriving at a community hospital, in coping with their trauma. After all, I had thought, such things just do not happen on Long Island. My reactions were similar to those I heard from Oklahoma City residents who also said that violence and terrorism "do not happen here." But they did, and they do.

THE IMPACT OF RANDOM VIOLENCE ON COMMUNITY PERCEPTIONS

We have all seen recent reports indicating that violence in the community is leveling off, with the exception of workplace violence. In some cases, such as New York City, the report is that such incidents have declined quite steeply. Why then do we still feel so anxious in light of these reported declines? This question was posed to me during a news interview about crime on Long Island and a general increase in community anxiety there, even in the face of lessened danger.

My answer had to do with the nature of violence in the community today. Although the *number* of violent incidents may be decreasing at present, the *nature* of these incidents seems more and more bent in the direction of randomness—and downright savagery. For example:

- Colin Ferguson, the Long Island Railroad mass murderer, did not kill one person he knew. He shot twenty strangers—killing six—while looking many of them in the eye as he pulled the trigger and then calmly reloaded his weapon.

- Nicole Simpson and Ron Goldman were not simply stabbed but viciously slashed numerous times in addition to having their throats cut.
- New York City police officer Lou Cosantino, while attempting to intervene in a fight among teenage youths, was reported to have been "beaten senseless" nearly to death by ten youths. His face required thirty screws and seven metal plates to be reconstructed.

Violence like this—so senseless and so gruesome—cannot help but be deeply disturbing. It undermines the trust we put in organized society. If we cannot feel secure on our streets, in our houses, at our shops, what is the point of organizing into a society at all? We must keep in mind that the nature of a crime is as important as its frequency. The kind of violence we see now is a direct attack on the very fabric of our communities. It is no wonder that statistics do not have the calming effect we might expect of them.

VIOLENCE IN THE WORKPLACE

Keep in mind that workplace violence was the exception to the general decline of violent incidents in the community. Violence in the workplace, although virtually unheard of a quarter of a century ago, has exploded in the last decade. Homicide in the workplace is increasing more rapidly than homicide in any other sector of society. Right now a majority of working adults have either witnessed, personally experienced, or seen in the media numerous violent acts in a workplace setting. Just as the term *carjacking* did not exist five or six years ago, similarly *workplace violence* is now all too familiar to us. (Even so, newspaper and media accounts reflect only the tip of the iceberg. Many incidents are never exposed because most companies make great efforts to keep them quiet and out of the media. This approach is representative of all the companies I have worked with as a consultant for trauma intervention in the aftermath of violence and/or serious workplace accidents.)

Nevertheless, workplace violence and homicide are the fastest-growing forms of violence in the United States, having doubled in the past ten years. In the workplace, violence is the second leading cause of death and the number one cause of death for women. A survey on workplace violence by the Society of Human Resource Management reported that more than one-third of the 479 respondents said incidents of violence occurred where they worked (fistfights, physical altercations, shootings, stabbings, and sexual assaults). Over half stated that between two and five acts of violence were committed in their workplace in the last five years.

The National Safe Work Institute reported that 112,000 workplace incidents occurred in 1992, costing American business $4.2 billion. As statistics for subsequent years are compiled, these numbers will most likely increase. In addition to the direct costs (medical and legal) of workplace violence, related costs also include a decline in company morale and consequent loss of productivity, increased absenteeism, higher employee turnover, and damage to a company's credibility and reputation.

We often think of violence in the workplace only in terms of fatal incidents; however, such incidents may include any of the following:

- Threats (in the form of letters, faxes, verbal confrontations)
- Vandalism (in buildings, rest rooms, parking lots)
- Equipment sabotage (e.g., tampering with computers)
- Personal conflict (fighting with coworkers, punching supervisors, assaults, shootings, stabbings, romantic obsession with a coworker)
- Family conflict (domestic violence, such as when a jealous husband arrives at a workplace and attacks his wife and possibly coworkers)
- Hostage taking (e.g., a former telephone company employee, angry about losing retirement benefits, took

several hostages and destroyed almost $10 million of equipment)

- Suicide (an employee in or near the workplace may commit suicide following a homicidal attack)
- Homicide (perhaps by a disgruntled employee or from someone outside, such as during holdups or random attacks—shootings at fast-food restaurants and convenience stores)

Such incidents often seriously affect workers who have witnessed or have been victims of workplace violence. The resulting traumas may include anxiety attacks, sleep and eating disorders, anger, irritability, difficulty in concentrating, alcohol and substance abuse, mood swings, psychosomatic disorders (e.g., stomach problems and headaches), feelings of helplessness and vulnerability (the sense that "no place is safe"), and flashbacks of the event. Such effects inevitably disrupt productivity and morale, and they adversely impact a company's bottom line. Workplace violence hurts—and it costs. Fatal incidents can be especially devastating to a company, as reported in a *Newsday* article (Associated Press, March 12, 1995):

Killing a Law Firm

Two years after a gunman invaded the high-rise offices of a San Francisco law firm and killed eight people, he's claimed another victim: the firm itself.

The 39-year-old Pettit & Martin firm is closing after suffering financial and personnel troubles since 1991. The number of lawyers at the firm has dropped from 240 in the late 1980s to 120. The firm made no mention of the killings when it announced its plans last week, but one partner said they were a severe blow. "I refuse to admit that a crazed gunman can defeat the will of a very good group of people, but it did have an effect on the spirit," the partner told the *San Francisco Examiner* on condition of anonymity. "The shooting forced the firm to grapple with a whole new set of emotions."

On July 1, 1993, Gian Luigi Ferri, a frustrated businessman who had had some dealings with the firm, opened fire in Pettit & Martin's offices. Eight people died and six were wounded before Ferri committed suicide. The firm, which has five offices on both coasts, is expected to close within two months.

The devastating impact of workplace violence has prompted some companies and organizations to develop prevention and intervention plans. Unfortunately, the majority of U.S. companies do not have any plans to deal with workplace violence. It often takes an incident and the resulting period of intervention counseling to prompt them to establish a plan for spotting potential trouble and heading it off.

ENVIRONMENTAL FACTORS ASSOCIATED WITH INCREASED WORKPLACE VIOLENCE

It is not by chance that workplace violence has escalated over the past few years. Although frustrated workers may respond violently to a variety of stress-related factors, three major environmental components appear to be related to the recent increase in such violent incidents:

1. Societal Factors

- So much violence is portrayed in the media that it leads at least to an acceptance, if not approval, of violence as a method for dealing with conflict.
- Increasingly available weapons
- Growing fascination with weapons as tools of power
- Societal factors that contribute to the breakdown of families and communities
- Violence as learned behavior in homes and on the streets
- Spillover of domestic violence into the workplace

2. *Economic Factors*

- Eroding economic climate, lower salaries, fewer benefits, higher costs
- Company "downsizing," reengineering, and use of subcontractors rather than full-time employees
- Lack of reentry opportunities for laid-off employees

3. *Management-Related Factors*

- Some firms employ outdated, impersonal managerial methods to deal with employee complaints; as a result, disillusionment and a lack of trust toward management may develop.
- Alleged wrongful discharge cases can stretch over years, which allows anger to build.

Although these environmental factors might contribute to someone's committing a violent act, violent feelings usually have deeper roots within a person's psyche. Understanding the characteristics of violence-prone people is one of the keys to identifying those individuals who might threaten or commit violence in the workplace.

IDENTIFYING THE POTENTIALLY VIOLENT PERSONALITY

There is no sure way to predict a person's behavior, so using a generic profile as a means of detecting potentially violent employees does have serious drawbacks. For example, people may be incorrectly identified as dangerous simply because they match a list of characteristics, whereas others may be erroneously overlooked because they do not match the list. Nevertheless, some signs should alert a company for possible trouble:

- A history of aggressive behavior. This sign is probably the best predictor of potential problems. The possibility of future violent behavior increases with each prior act.

- Serious family problems and conflicts. True, most people have problems of one sort or another, but expressions of extreme desperation, severe financial problems, or domestic turmoil (especially if long-standing) are signs of possible violence.
- Continually blaming others for problems and unwillingness to take responsibility for one's own actions
- Frequent anger or hostility
- Lack of control of impulses; flare-ups and aggressive behavior toward coworkers, often involving physical contact such as pushing or punching
- Abuse of drugs and/or alcohol. Alcohol and certain drugs create paranoia and aggressive behavior, interfere with reasoning ability, and lessen social inhibition; the marginal individual is pushed over the edge.
- Possession of or access to weapons
- Social isolation; a loner
- Overly suspicious/paranoid behavior
- Chronic work-related conflicts and perceived injustices. An individual may be unable to take criticism of job performance, hold a grudge against a supervisor, verbalize hope for something to happen to a coworker, or frequently file unreasonable grievances and lawsuits.
- Intimidation of others. This behavior may involve harassing phone calls, stalking behavior, or romantic obsession with a coworker who does not return the interest.
- Threats toward company or another employee

Keep in mind that the presence of one or more of these signs does not mean an employee is a menace. Still, they should prompt management to stay alert for potential problems.

Certain other traits are frequently cited, but they are too vague to be of much help—for instance, "white male, thirties to forties" (the singer Selena was murdered by the female head of her fan club), "low self-esteem," "sees company as family" (more likely to derive sense of identity from job, as other areas of life may be lacking satisfaction).

Although it is good to be aware of these warning signs of potential trouble, it is also crucial for supervisors to sense any early indications that an employee is undergoing undue emotional stress. Such awareness may help managers guide an employee into obtaining professional help, thus averting a more serious problem later. Some of the signs indicating that an employee may be running into emotional trouble include these:

1. Sudden changes from usual behavior
2. Increased anxiety and irritability
3. Mention of sleep disturbances
4. Excessive drinking or drug use
5. Noted sexual problems, including harassing behavior
6. Excessive altercations with others
7. Becoming more accident prone
8. Becoming argumentative or developing feelings of being persecuted
9. Talk of physical complaints
10. Talk of home problems
11. Loss of interest and confidence in life or work
12. Depression, withdrawal, and comments about suicide

Certainly, extreme, agitated depression is a red flag and may lead to self-destructive behavior and possible suicide, homicide, or both.

Typical Signs of Depression

- Expressions of despair ("I just don't care anymore. What difference does it make?")
- A slowed work pace
- Perpetual blank, sad, or frowning expression
- Distractability and sluggish decision making
- Increased apathy; lack of motivation
- Social withdrawal
- Excessive self-condemnation
- Self-destructive behavior (such as suicide attempt)
- Feelings of hopelessness

- Sense of helplessness
- Inappropriate guilt or shame
- Unkempt physical appearance

Emotional difficulties can be viewed along a continuum, from mild signs of emotional depression to more serious impairments or personality disorders. Two of the more common personality disorders among violent individuals are discussed next.

Antisocial Personality Disorder

This disorder is more common in males than females. People with antisocial personality disorder tend to be irritable and aggressive, with track records of fighting outside the home and domestic violence inside the home. They may engage in harassing others and steal or destroy property. They have little regard for the truth, are impulsive in action, and may own a weapon. Generally, antisocial individuals will have little remorse about wrongdoing and seek to justify their violent behavior. These individuals do not have long-lasting, warm, and responsible relationships with family or friends. Antisocial personality individuals will have a history of quitting jobs without having another position available, or they may be unemployed for extended periods of time even if they were offered employment. When they are employed, it is not unusual for them to be frequently absent from work without a justified explanation.

Borderline Personality Disorder

The essential features of this disorder are instability in interpersonal relationships and self-image, as well as lack of appropriate boundaries. These individuals may be uncertain concerning career choice, value systems, and long-term goals. Such individuals experience severe mood shifts with inappropriate anger often displayed in repeated fights. These people, like those suffering from antisocial behavior disorder, are very impulsive and can be easily irritated. Excellent manipulators of people, borderline personality individuals may fear a real or imagined abandonment by others, and they are not averse to making suicidal threats to avoid the perceived loss. Borderline personality individuals, much like self-absorbed narcissistic personality individuals, are preoccupied with themselves and have little compunction about using others to achieve their purposes. Not all individuals with borderline or antisocial personality disorders will become violent, but these conditions are hardly rare and do bear watching.

Also, on the more extreme end of the continuum are individuals who suffer from *psychosis,* which is characterized by a loss of contact with reality, sometimes referred to as a "thought disorder." Thought disorders are often reflected in poor associations in conversations, flat facial expressions, and poor insight. Psychoses may include schizophrenia, paranoia, and/or delusional thinking. The emotionally disturbed or impaired employee needs immediate counseling from a qualified mental health professional. Referral for psychological help is not the job for a manager but is more appropriately handled by the human resources department and/or an employee assistance program.

CRISIS MANAGEMENT

The first step toward heading off the potential for violence in the workplace is to admit that it may be possible. If an emotionally disturbed employee leads you to believe a violent episode may be in the offing, a strict discipline session is *not* the answer. A more effective approach is to offer counseling services for this person—and not under the threat of termination—rather than trigger possible impulsive, angry behavior with a harsh tone. Other types of violence, however, such as fighting or harassment, should be dealt with through more typical disciplinary measures. Consultation with a mental health professional who is a specialist in dealing with conflict and violence should be a high priority in such instances.

When a violent incident occurs, the aftermath takes a toll on the psychological health of affected individuals and their families. In the wake of a traumatic violent incident, it is important to contact the trauma intervention team (as previously designated or developed by the company) as soon as possible. Intervention should ideally take place twenty-four to seventy-two hours after the incident.

Reactions of employees who have been victims of workplace violence and trauma may include anxiety attacks, sleep and eating disorders, anger, irritability, difficulty concentrating, alcohol and substance abuse, mood swings, psychosomatic disorders such as stomach problems and headaches, feelings of helplessness and vulnerability—"no place is safe"—as well as flashbacks of the event.

One of the most important factors in the recovery process is the nature of the help received by the victims immediately after the incident. Traditional counseling and psychotherapy are not appropriate at this point. Inappropriate intervention, no matter how well intended, can exacerbate an already tense and difficult situation, producing more harm than good. Specialized psychological help addressing critical incident stress is required to lay the foundation for recovery and to prevent the onset of posttraumatic stress disorder. Unfortunately, I have witnessed well-intended but inappropriate help in the form of grief or bereavement counseling being done for companies by mental health professionals. This approach is inappropriate because the grieving process does not even begin until further down the road and because it does not address the unique issues related to violence.

Distinguishing between Short-Term and Long-Term Trauma

The specialty of *trauma psychology* (a term originated by E. Carll, 1991) considers the psychological aftermath of violence, as well as disasters, crises, and accidents, and the resulting acute and posttraumatic stress. As indicated in *DSM-IV,* the diagnosis of posttraumatic stress disorder is made if the symptoms (such as recurrent and intrusive recollections of the event, flashbacks, avoidance, and increased arousal) continue for more than one month. However, the recognition that these symptoms occur within days to weeks after a traumatic event and are also severe enough to require immediate psychological intervention prompted the additional diagnosis of acute stress disorder to be included in *DSM-IV*. *Acute stress disorder* is defined as a disturbance lasting a minimum of two days and a maximum of four weeks and occurring within four weeks of the traumatic event. Those of us who have provided emergency mental health services on-site and immediately after a disaster or crisis are especially aware of the usefulness of the diagnosis of acute stress disorder in establishing the need for immediate and short-term intervention. Frequently, short-term intervention is referred to as critical incident stress debriefing, critical incident stress management, or critical incident stress intervention.

What Is Critical Incident Stress Intervention?

Critical incident stress intervention (CISI; a term originated by E. Carll, 1992) encompasses immediate services (critical incident stress debriefings) as well as short- and longer-term follow-up as needed. *Critical incident stress debriefings* (CISDs) are very different from traditional psychotherapy. They are based on a psychoeducational model that assumes normal people are experiencing normal reactions to an abnormal event or incident. A *critical incident* is defined as any event that has the capacity to overwhelm a person's usual coping ability. Such events vary from person to person, and reactions are incident specific.

Critical incident stress debriefings are confidential structured group meetings (although they can be conducted individually) that focus on ventilating emotions and other reactions generated by a critical incident. The optimal size of a CISD is ten to fourteen individuals, although flexibility is necessary in addressing special circumstances or needs. The process can take approximately two to four hours and is ideally conducted within twenty-four to seventy-two hours of a critical event, with follow-up debriefings conducted as needed. However, CISDs conducted a week or more after an incident may also prove beneficial.

A debriefing has four major goals:

1. Reduce the impact of the critical event.
2. Accelerate the normal recovery process.
3. Provide education and stress management strategies.
4. Assess the need for possible follow-up counseling and psychotherapy, which may be needed in a small percentage of cases.

I cannot overemphasize the importance of using outside trauma specialists for consultation. After a violent incident, everyone in the company is affected (i.e., secondary traumatization). Using company staff raises employees' concerns about confidentiality, a possible adverse effect on their jobs, and unfavorable information going into their personnel files. In my experience, when we counselors ask the employees whether a company human resources (HR) person may sit in on a group debriefing, in all instances the employees preferred that no one from management be part of the group intervention. This setup also takes pressure off the HR person because things may be said during the course of the group meeting that may be embarrassing to the employee or even to the HR person. This session may lead to awkward interactions in the future.

Moreover, if a concern has been raised about an employee who is making verbal threats, an expert in workplace violence can help assess the situation and offer recommendations that will prevent escalation. Again, this may take pressure off HR persons, as they need to maintain ongoing relationships with the people involved.

In large-scale incidents such as the Oklahoma City bombing, the World Trade Center bombing, or the Long Island Railroad shootings, the community at large is vicariously traumatized and should be considered secondary victims. Public education through the media can be instrumental in facilitating the community's recovery from the trauma. The goals of public education are twofold:

1. Help people understand what they are and will be experiencing emotionally.
2. Teach coping strategies to be used in the days, weeks, and months to come.

Developing a Violence Prevention Plan

A workplace violence prevention plan should be comprehensive and include many elements in addition to a trauma action plan to deal with the direct aftermath of an incident. Preplanning is vital. Without it, for example, think how difficult it might be to find trauma/violence specialists in the twenty-four hours following an incident and to have them ready to intervene immediately. Following are some pertinent strategies to help in setting up a comprehensive prevention plan:

1. Adopt a "zero tolerance" approach when dealing with workplace violence. Make all employees aware that any threats or acts of violence will not be tolerated.
2. Form a management team to develop, review, and implement policies dealing with workplace violence. The team should include senior management, human resources personnel, a mental health consultant who is an expert in workplace violence, legal counsel, security, and any other related personnel.
3. Training is crucial to prevention. Conduct training seminars on recognizing and dealing with workplace violence. They should include training courses on detecting early warning signs of potentially violent behavior and on responding to and investigating an incident of workplace violence. Contrary to popular belief, violent employees do not just snap without warning or clues; usually, multiple clues have been observed by a number

of people. Coworkers and supervisors who are observant and have been trained to know what to look for can often see the violence coming.

4. The natural reaction of most people to a threatening statement is to make light of it or turn away. It is not the lack of clues that generally causes the problem but the unwillingness of fellow workers and supervisors to recognize such behaviors as warning signs and to report them to management for evaluation and action.

5. Develop a method for workers to make confidential tips about knowledge of threats or impending violence. Often employees may be concerned about possible retribution or other problems arising from involvement.

6. Develop crisis procedures and a trauma action plan that can be put into action immediately to respond to an incident of workplace violence.

7. Improve security measures, and develop a working relationship with law enforcement authorities.

8. Prevent workplace violence through consistent enforcement of workplace rules and the use of proper pre-screening, employee assistance programs (EAPs), and medical and mental health resources.

9. Develop public relations procedures and strategies to cope with the media spotlight following incidents of violence.

10. Prevent workplace violence through ongoing training. Training should include stress management, conflict resolution, coping with difficult people, coping with change in the workplace, and dealing with sexual harassment and domestic violence.

A July 1993 survey of six hundred full-time workers, conducted by Northwestern National Life Insurance Company, found that more than 15 percent of those surveyed had been physically attacked at some time during their working life. More than 21 percent said they had been threatened with physical harm. Obviously, it's best to deal with a problem before it escalates.

DOMESTIC VIOLENCE IN THE WORKPLACE

With more women in the workplace than ever before, abusive husbands and boyfriends may stalk spouses and girlfriends and eventually show up at the workplace. Homicide is the number one cause of death for women in the workplace. A recent U.S. Department of Labor (1996) study revealed that in 17 percent of these homicides, the alleged assailants were current or former husbands or boyfriends. Information about workplace and hours are easily obtained. Recent news reports, such as those following, spotlight this increasing problem:

> The highly publicized case of the February 1996 murder of Galina Komar at her office in a Queens, New York, car dealership, by her estranged boyfriend, Benito Oliver (who then committed suicide), brought the problem of domestic violence in the workplace to public attention. When it was learned that a judge had recently released Oliver after he had violated an order of protection, with a two-year history of stalking, beating, and threatening Komar, the public and legal community were vehemently critical of the judge.

> On October 20, 1995, a gunman shot and killed his loan officer wife at the bank where she was employed and then shot himself to death. The couple was estranged, and she had filed for a divorce. Seven employees in the bank had taken refuge within the bank vault before escaping.

> On December 19, 1995, a man fatally shot a female coworker at a Chrysler assembly plant in Detroit, Michigan, and then fatally shot himself. He and the coworker had been dating for several months.

In addition to the direct cost of such incidents, domestic violence in the workplace costs employers $3 to $5 billion annually because of worker absenteeism. Abusive husbands and boyfriends harass 74 percent of employed battered women at work, either in person or over the telephone, causing 56 percent of them to be late for work at least five times a month, 28 percent to leave early at least five days a month, and 54 percent to miss at least three full days of work a month (Friedman & Cooper, 1987). A survey (Roper, Starch Worldwide Survey for Liz Claiborne, Inc., 1994) of senior executives of Fortune 1,000 companies found that 66 percent of the executives believed that a company's financial performance would benefit from addressing the issue of domestic violence among its employees. The survey also revealed that almost 60 percent of corporate leaders believe domestic violence is a major problem, and 40 percent are personally aware of employees in their companies who have been affected by domestic violence. In addition, a recent survey of corporate security directors revealed that more than 90 percent of those surveyed were aware of more than three incidents in which men stalked women employees, and 94 percent said that domestic violence is a high security problem at their companies.

Clearly, companies need to develop workplace policies that address domestic disputes. For example, I have recommended to organizations that as a matter of procedure they should inquire whether employees have orders of protection against family members or others. Not only is this step helpful for security purposes, but it may be a deterrent if violence-prone individuals know they will be arrested if they show up at their spouses' workplace.

Elements of a Comprehensive Workplace Domestic Violence Program

A comprehensive workplace violence program should address domestic violence issues, with the following specific features:

- Employee training programs should be designed to teach managers to identify victims of domestic violence at work and how to direct them to available services such as

EAPs and/or community services. All new managers should be required to attend the training as part of their orientation.

- Company leadership can demonstrate support for addressing issues of domestic violence by having all employees attend awareness seminars, which would include recognizing signs and learning what to say to help a co-worker who may be a victim of domestic violence.

- Security measures should be improved to address stalking of employees and special needs of victims of domestic violence. These may include modified work schedules, relocation of work areas or work sites, availability of identifying information and photographs of the perpetrator/stalker to security and reception areas, limiting information available by telephone about employees' schedules or whereabouts, and leave of absence in high-risk situations.

- Benefit packages should be sensitive to the needs of victims of violence, such as leave policies enabling women to get time off to go to court.

- Official company programs should promote fund-raising for community domestic violence services, volunteerism, and awards to employees who develop innovative programs that benefit the company.

- Informative articles addressing domestic violence can be included in company newsletters and publications.

- Information about domestic violence resources should be readily available through not only an employee assistance program but also other strategic areas (i.e., hot line numbers posted in the company cafeteria and lavatories).

- An immediate, effective trauma intervention response plan and team should be available to deal with the aftermath of a crisis. Even with the best readiness and prevention plans in place, however, violence may sometimes still occur.

CONCLUSION

Unfortunately, most companies do not have a plan in place to deal with an event of workplace violence. Violence prevention plans and policies are in the same position as sexual harassment policies were five years ago. What is necessary is a comprehensive plan that includes prevention strategies. Training should be offered to recognize impending and escalating problems as well as develop skills in managing and defusing conflict, anger, and stress. Sometimes, however, even with the best readiness and prevention plans in place, violence may still occur. It is then essential to have a fast and effective trauma intervention plan in place to deal with the aftermath.

With appropriate planning and intervention, the morale, productivity, legal, financial, and corporate image problems arising from workplace violence can be minimized. A preparedness plan will benefit not only the corporate bottom line and safety, but also the lives of employees and the community.

3

DOMESTIC AND INTIMATE RELATIONSHIP VIOLENCE

ELIZABETH K. CARLL, Ph.D.

Every fifteen seconds a woman is beaten by her husband or boy-friend (Federal Bureau of Investigation [FBI], 1991). We heard this statistic on TV over and over during the long O. J. Simpson trial and its attendant talk show debates. It is certainly attention grab-bing, and it graphically illustrates the magnitude of the domestic violence problem. However, despite enormous media attention, we find that attitudes about the devastating consequences of do-mestic violence change very slowly. For example, even at the height of the media frenzy over the O. J. Simpson trial, a Suffolk County, New York, judge refused an assistant district attorney's request to impose $5,000 bail on a Brentwood, New York, man accused of raping his ex-girlfriend (with whom he had lived for six years prior to their breakup) at knifepoint. The district court judge instead set bail at $200 (Nash, 1994).

It was the routine nature of the incident that weighed most heavily in the judge's decision. The assistant DA, citing the "vio-lent circumstances" surrounding the incident and the fact that the perpetrator was still on probation from prior drug sales con-victions, requested that bail be set at $5,000. The judge, however, noted that the woman told police that her ex-boyfriend had also held the knife to himself, threatening self-harm. "The allegations are that there were violent acts, but this is a situation I've seen in other cases," stated the judge. "I don't think it's appropriate to hold the defendant till trial." Such casual acceptance and minimization of the crime of domestic violence by our judicial system cannot help but be deeply disturbing and send a chilling message to those who look to the courts for justice and protection.

Other examples abound. An Associated Press story that ran in several newspapers (e.g., *Newsday,* October 19, 1994) told about a Maryland man who shot and killed his wife because she was unfaithful. The judge imposed the minimum sentence of eighteen months' jail time for the murder and was reported to have stated, "I seriously wonder how many men married five, four years would have the strength to walk away without inflicting some corporal punishment. . . . I am forced to impose a sentence . . . only because I must do it to keep the system honest." Such trivialization of domestic violence against women has long-standing cultural roots in many societies, including the United States. Until the early 1970s, New Mexico and Texas law stated that a man who caught his wife committing adultery and killed her could claim justifiable homicide and be acquitted. The laws allowing such a defense are modern versions of old English common law, whereby a man who killed his wife was doing away with his own property, while a wife who killed her husband, the king of the manor, had committed treason. Considering how lightly society views the problem of domestic violence, regardless of many protestations to the contrary, it is understandable that victims are not quick to seek help. But the problem remains. Domestic violence is in fact the most underreported crime in the United States, and battering is the leading cause of injury to women, exceeding muggings, auto accidents, and cancer deaths combined (U.S. Senate Committee on the Judiciary, 1992).

Even today the seeds of old English law are still evident. Although some battered women who kill their abusers are acquitted in subsequent trials, those who do plead guilty or are convicted are often sentenced to lengthy prison sentences. In a study of one hundred battered women homicide cases, thirty-one were convicted of murder, with twelve receiving life sentences (Ewing, 1987). Ewing (1987) further states that despite abundant evidence that many battered women were severely physically and psychologically abused by the men they eventually killed, they were convicted of murder or manslaughter even though they pleaded self-defense. Other researchers (Dutton, Hohnecker, Halle, & Burghardt, 1994; Ferraro, 1993; Stout, 1991; Walker, 1989) have reported similar findings.

THE MAGNITUDE OF THE DOMESTIC VIOLENCE PROBLEM

To get a full picture of how pervasive domestic violence is, we must remember that it includes violence and abuse between not only family members but also extramarital heterosexual partners, same-gender couples, and adult and adolescent dating partners. Obviously, a term such as *intimate relationship violence* would more aptly describe the parameters of domestic violence. Moreover, even though domestic violence does have an impact on children, the violence and abuse directed specifically at children is generally defined under a separate category, *child abuse*. Many excellent books (Barnett, Miller-Perrin, & Perrin, 1997; Bolton & Bolton, 1987; Hampton, Gullotta, Adams, Potter, & Weissberg, 1993; Van Hasselt, Morrison, Bellack, & Herson, 1988) are available that provide a comprehensive theoretical analysis of the topic, including child abuse, elder abuse, and ethnic/cultural considerations. The focus of this chapter is a pragmatic overview and understanding of abuse and violence in heterosexual intimate relationships.

So widespread is domestic violence that it evoked a warning from the former surgeon general of the United States, C. Everett Koop, identifying violence as the number one health risk to adult women in the United States (Schornstein, 1997). Battering is the single most frequent reason that women seek attention at hospital emergency wards, and it is the largest major cause of injury to women, accounting for 25 percent of female suicide attempts and 4,000 homicides per year (Holtz & Furniss, 1993). Domestic violence is so common in our society that one woman in four is likely to be abused by a partner during her lifetime (Glazer, 1993). Others have put these estimates at even higher levels.

CHARACTERISTICS OF ABUSIVE AND VIOLENT RELATIONSHIPS

We cannot formulate appropriate intervention strategies or prevent abusive and violent relationships until we have a clearer picture of the characteristics of such relationships. Initially, it is essential to identify and rectify our commonly held misconceptions about battering. We must then grasp the pattern in the cycle of abuse, become aware of the personality characteristics of batterers, and understand the psychological reactions of battered women and why they often stay in such relationships. (Please note that although a small percentage of men are battered, the vast majority of battering and violence incidents—96 percent—are directed at women. Thus, this discussion of domestic violence and research cited in it will be directed specifically to the issues of battered women.)

Those of us who have worked with abused clients recognize the devastating effects of violence. We understand that no woman wants to be battered, mutilated, or murdered. In fact, many women go to great lengths to avoid violent men who may continue to stalk them. (Because stalking is such a serious and frequent characteristic of a variety of violent relationships, it is addressed in detail in a subsequent chapter.) Following are some of the more readily—and not readily—identifiable characteristics of abusive relationships:

- Violent relationships encompass more than just physical abuse, including a constellation of abusive behaviors. Physical abuse includes pushing, shoving, pulling, spitting, hitting, kicking, punching, as well as assault with any type of weapon. Other abusive behaviors may include emotional abuse, which involves things like name-calling, denigration, and humiliation. There may also be coercion and threats, such as threats to harm the victim's family members or friends if she tells others or refuses to cooperate, as well as other forms of intimidation. Not infrequently, the batterer attempts to make light of the problem, and his own aggressive behavior, by blaming the victim for provoking incidents that result in violence.

- Sexual abuse/assault is frequently present. Half of all rapes of women over thirty are part of the battering syndrome, and marital rape is much more common than generally thought. Sexual assault also includes date/acquaintance rapes. The frequency and magnitude of the problem of sexual assault and rape has resulted in a growing body of research and knowledge, including psychological, sociological, cross-cultural, and feminist theory that would warrant a separate volume on this topic. Therefore the reader is referred to several excellent books written in this area (Brownmiller, 1975; Calhoun & Atkeson, 1991; Dobash & Dobash, 1979; Finkelhor & Yllo, 1985; Koss & Harvey, 1991; Levy, 1991; Ward, 1995).

- In a domestic violence situation, the batterer often attempts to isolate the victim from her friends and family and from all who might potentially provide support.

- Stalking is not unusual and is often intended to intimidate the victim as well as maintain control through continuous surveillance of the victim's activities.

DEBUNKING MYTHS ABOUT ABUSIVE RELATIONSHIPS

In addition to sensitizing ourselves to the signs that characterize an abusive situation, we need to look past some of the misconceptions, half-truths, and myths that cloud both men's and women's understandings about violent relationships.

Myth 1: Women Can Always Leave an Abusive Relationship

Perhaps the most commonly held myth is that a battered woman can always leave her home and thereby end an intolerable relationship. It seems logical. If the conditions of a relationship are so bad, why not leave? Terminating an abusive relationship, however desirable such a termination might be, is a difficult and complex process. It involves so many factors and considerations that we will devote a full discussion to this problem in the next section.

Myth 2: Once a Victim, Always a Victim

Although several women in the Walker (1989) study had a series of violent relationships, most had learned to recognize the telltale signs of abuse and were extremely cautious about whom they dated or became involved with. Women who received beneficial intervention rarely married another batterer. My experience has been that women who have been able to extricate themselves from a violent relationship are very relieved and not eager to become involved in another relationship too soon.

Myth 3: Battered Women Are Masochistic

A common belief is that only women who "like it and deserve it" remain in a battering relationship, therefore, these women must derive some satisfaction through being beaten by the men they love. As we have seen, however, most women in an abusive relationship want the abuse to stop and derive no joy from it, but because this view is such a common stereotype, many battered women begin to wonder whether they, indeed, are masochistic. This is rarely the case, but because the belief is so prevalent, it presents still another stumbling block for them to overcome in order to free themselves from the relationship.

Myth 4: Battered Women Bring It upon Themselves

Research shows that batterers lose self-control because of their own internal reasons, *not* because of what the women did or did not do. There is nothing a person can say or do that justifies violence. This myth is mostly a self-justifying ploy of abusers.

Myth 5: Batterers Display Violence in All of Their Relationships

Only a small number, about 20 percent, of the men who batter women are violent to others outside their home; on the contrary, they are generally not violent in other aspects of their lives. Often, they may hold responsible positions and may be considered respected members of the community.

Myth 6: Long-Standing Battering Relationships Can Change for the Better

Relationships that are based on the man having power and control over the woman are stubbornly resistant to an equal power-sharing arrangement. Often the abuser is not motivated to change but only motivated to maintain the relationship. Even with the best of help, such relationships usually do not become battering-free. At best, violent assaults are reduced in frequency and severity. Even if the physical abuse stops, the emotional abuse frequently continues. The long-term prospects for changing and salvaging a prolonged abusive relationship are not good.

WHY SHE STAYS: THE BARRIERS TO LEAVING

If the myths about abusive relationships are just that—myths—then why do so many women stay in these relationships for long periods of time? To be of any help to the victims of an abusive relationship, we must understand why the seemingly immediate, simple answer—"Leave"—is rarely immediate and never simple.

Looking at the situation practically, we must see that, in the absence of professional intervention and counseling, many battered women have no place to go and no means of survival outside the structure of their marriage/relationship. Such women often have small children to care for, whom they would fear leaving at home alone with the father, especially after a violent outburst. Even if they flee to a shelter temporarily with the children, many of these women find they must return home sooner or later as they cannot financially support themselves and the children apart from the relationship.

As important as the financial issues are, equally critical psychological factors explain why women do not leave. Keep in mind that many of these relationships initially may have been violence-free and not even perceived as abusive. Gradually, however, the husbands or boyfriends became increasingly more controlling, then verbally and emotionally abusive, and, eventually, physically violent. Also, within some abusive relationships periods of time occur between violent episodes that are mutually satisfying, that recall earlier happy times in the relationship, and that foster hope for improvement. The victim is thus yanked back and forth between hope and despair. We call this the *cycle of abuse,* and Walker (1989) describes the three stages of an episode of violence that help explain this deadly cycle that entraps so many women.

Stage 1: **The buildup.** During this initial stage, minor battering and pushing occur. She may attempt to calm him, take on a nurturing role, and/or become compliant. Although she may feel anger, she rationalizes the situation and blames outside forces, such as unemployment or job stress for his abusive behavior.

Stage 2: **The blowup.** His tension builds to an eruption of violence with acute battering and uncontrollable rage. He justifies his behavior by citing petty annoyances, such as her nagging, that caused him to batter.

Stage 3:   The honeymoon. The couple attempts to put the relationship back on track. He may appear charming, loving, contrite, and displays kind behavior. He begs forgiveness and offers gifts. Both rationalize the situation (i.e., drinking, work pressures, etc.) as the cause of the blowup. It is this stage that perpetuates the cycle of abuse because it fosters the victim's hope by providing her with a glimpse of the man she married. It leads both partners to rationalize the situation and believe they can overcome their problems if only they stick together. During this stage, women who have enlisted professional help often abandon support groups or counselors, drop charges, drop orders of protection, or back down on separation or divorce proceedings in the belief that the situation has reversed itself.

In my experience, as well as that of other professionals, this third stage is an especially difficult time in which to provide intervention. This phase often results in considerable frustration for attorneys, therapists, and the judicial system, who see their efforts derailed. They see, as the couple does not or will not, that the problem has *not* been resolved and that the cycle will be repeated. Yet during this phase, many (but not all) batterers are often described by their victims as attentive, sensitive, affectionate, and remorseful, and thus they should be given another chance. It is only after numerous repetitions of this cycle that many women are finally driven to seriously consider leaving or to begin seeking help. According to Browne (1987), battered women return home on the average of six to seven times before finally leaving for good.

We must understand that this enumeration of the stages of the cycle of abuse is only an overview of a very complex series of events. For example, the length of the stages and the transition periods vary in each individual case. Moreover, some women who have lived through many repetitions of this cycle may become both psychologically and physically worn out. *The honeymoon stage may not even occur,* the only relief being a temporary absence of violence. In other situations, the batterer may not show remorse for his behavior but only use threats, intimidation, and violence to keep the victim from leaving. She may not see any light at the end of the tunnel, and in her despairing state she may lack the confidence and self-esteem required to extricate herself from the abuse.

A number of theories explaining abusive relationships have been cited in the literature. The theory of *traumatic bonding and intermittent reinforcement* developed by Dutton and Painter (1981) refers to the formation of strong emotional ties between two individuals, one of whom is abusive and intermittently intimidates, harasses, beats, threatens, and abuses the other. Examples of these relationships include hostage/captor (often described as the Stockholm syndrome), abusive parent/child relationships, and membership in certain cults.

According to the theory of *learned helplessness* (Seligman, 1975; Seligman et al., 1968), an abused individual becomes passive and immobilized because she feels that her response will change the situation and that she has no power to extricate herself. As a result, the victim becomes more immobilized, fearful, and depressed. However, it is important to keep in mind that in certain violent relationships, this type of behavior may be more accurately described as "learned self-preservation," as the woman is keenly aware that an attempt to leave may well trigger violence, even lethal violence. Many excellent books (Browne, 1987; Dobash & Dobash, 1979; Ewing, 1987; Pence & Paymar, 1986), are available that discuss various theories in detail. Walker's cycle of violence theory is especially useful as it describes the abusive relationship in terms of a predictable continuum.

In addition, for some individuals, continued living with violence, terror, and stress may result in the development of the symptoms of *posttraumatic stress disorder* (PTSD), described as part of the "battered woman syndrome" (Walker, 1989). These may include anxiety, depression, a sense of hopelessness, sleeping difficulties, irritability and anger, difficulty in concentrating, shame, and embarrassment. The psychological reactions to chronic abuse characteristics of battered women are similar to the PTSD displayed by prisoners of war and other crisis survivors. Women in such a state may well need professional help to muster the will and strength to act on their own behalf. It does not mean they want to stay in the situation; it means they need help before they can act to change it.

Economic dependence and the psychological effects of the cycle of violence, fostering, as they often do, hope and optimism that things can get better, are significant factors in persuading women to stay in battering relationships. Several other reasons, however, also play an important role in the decision to remain, including these:

- **Family and business pressure to keep family together.** Such pressures put a premium on staying in the relationship and working out the problems, whatever they may be. Some families may not even accept the idea of divorce. They may point out that other family members have lived with abusive partners and kept the marriage intact. Also, in many cases, depriving the children of the chance to live with their father may be viewed as far more negative than enduring intermittent or chronic abuse.

- **Obligation to uphold marital vows regardless of the circumstances.** For some, it is essential to their vow to remain married "for better or for worse, until death do us part." Unfortunately, in some cases that is precisely what happens.

- **Fear.** He threatens to kill her and her children if she leaves. He may also threaten to kill himself.

- **Low self-esteem.** She believes that the problems in the relationship are her fault and that she is the cause of his problems. Therefore, she deserves to be treated badly. Even if she could leave, no one else would want her.

- **Embarrassment and shame.** She does not want anyone to know how she is being treated. She does not want to reveal humiliating details in court.
- **Fear of being alone.** Not having anyone is worse than being with someone who is abusive.
- **Minimizing the violence.** This is a form of solving a problem by pretending it is not there. "It is really not so bad; after all, at times he can be nice."
- **Learned helplessness.** She feels paralyzed, overwhelmed, and unable to extricate herself. She sees no way out. She may never have seen herself as exercising any control over her life in the past. She does not believe that others will help her because they may not believe her or, if they do, they will blame her for the problems, as he does.
- **Isolation.** The batterer exercises strict control: he monitors or prohibits phone calls and mail and prevents her from seeing friends or family. As a result, she may be isolated and without a support system. The abuser frequently controls access to money and may pressure her not to work to keep her from being able to become independent.
- **Fear of going to court to prosecute him for his violent behavior.** She believes that testifying will trigger his violence and the judicial system will not be able to protect her.

Obviously, like war, an abusive marriage/relationship is easier to begin than to end. "Just leave" may be the answer, but much counseling and nourishing work may need to be done before this solution can be practically implemented. Those who want to help women in an abusive situation—professionals, friends, relations—must be aware of this and act accordingly. In addition, these helpers—and women in general—should sensitize themselves to the signs that characterize a potential abuser.

WARNING SIGNS OF POTENTIAL VIOLENCE

How can one identify the warning signs of a potentially abusive and violent relationship? Listed here are characteristics that, when displayed by a husband/partner, indicate that he may well be disposed to develop abusive and violent behavior.

- **Excessive jealousy**—may involve monitoring her behavior to make sure she does not become interested in someone else. The monitoring may take such forms as frequent calls to the wife, actual surveillance, and car mileage checks. Accusations of flirting and affairs are common. There is also jealousy over time spent with friends and family. Abusers will state that jealousy is a sign of love; in reality, jealousy is a sign of insecurity, possessiveness, and lack of trust.
- **Blaming others for his problems**—claims that problems at work, financial problems, unemployment, and the like, are always caused by someone else, often his partner.
- **Blaming others for his feelings and using emotional blackmail**—includes statements such as "If you wouldn't nag me, I wouldn't get so mad" and "If you loved me, you would do what I ask."
- **Difficulty in controlling his temper**—is frequently hypersensitive. He is easily insulted and explodes in rage over minor daily frustrations.
- **Controlling and domineering behavior**—questions intensely about where she went and whom she spoke with. He may eventually want to make decisions about the way she dresses and what she should buy. He often restricts her access to finances, making her ask for money for every little expense. Eventually she may even have to

ask permission to go out of the house, even for daily errands.

- **History of violence within his family**—has personal experience with an abusive home. The man may have witnessed his mother and father being violent with each other or his siblings. He may also have been the victim of violence. His family may have resolved problems by using violence as the deciding vote.

- **Rigid sex roles**—expects that women will be subordinate to men. He may expect women not to work outside the home and does not view women as equal in ability or intelligence to men.

- **Verbal abuse**—makes denigrating and cruel comments, name-calling and cursing. The abuser may tell her that no one else would want her and that she could not function without him.

- **History of violence/battering in previous relationships**—may excuse his behavior by citing situational factors or by insisting that his previous partner made him do it. This trait is a red flag warning. Abusive behavior is not a function of situation variables but of internal personality characteristics. Remember that the best predictor of future behavior is past behavior.

It is equally important for women to be able to recognize the signs that their relationship is beginning to slide into an abusive one. The following four behavior traits actually indicate the beginning of battering in a relationship and may signal the onset of more extreme violence to come. Unfortunately, many women and men do not recognize these behaviors as battering.

- **Throwing, breaking, or striking objects**—doing this to create fear. The implication is, of course, to avoid making him any angrier—or else. Destroying his partner's prized possessions may be retaliation for not doing what he wants.

- **Abusing pets**—mistreating, deliberately hurting, or even killing family pets. Abusing animals can result from displaced aggression upon a weaker being. The abuse can also be the deliberate infliction of psychological pain stemming from the loss of a beloved animal. Also implied is the threat that if he becomes angry enough, perhaps she will be his next target. The relationship between family violence and pet abuse has gained recent attention in research literature (Ascione, 1993; Beck, 1981; Besharov, 1990; Dutton, 1992; Gelles & Strauss, 1988; Renzetti, 1992).
- **Making threats of violence**—intending to control the woman. Statements exemplifying such threats are "If you don't shut up, I'll make you"; "I'll knock your block off"; and "If you do that, I'll break your neck."
- **Using force during an argument**—for example, holding a woman down or against a wall or pushing or shoving to prevent her from leaving when shouting at her or to intimidate her into acceptance of his demands. Having crossed the line to physically intimidating her, it is only a matter of time before he escalates the violence to more brutal levels.

If women can spot such tendencies toward violence and excessive control early in a relationship, they may be able to seek help and counseling before a full-blown abusive situation develops.

IMPACT OF FAMILY AND COMMUNITY VIOLENCE ON CHILDREN

Studies estimate 30 to 70 percent of men who batter their wives also abuse their children (Hilton, 1992; Straus et al., 1980; Walker, 1984). The abuse can be direct, as in physical or sexual abuse directed at the child personally, or it may constitute emotional abuse resulting from exposing the child to violence against a parent or other family member.

We also see that violence against children often begets violence *among* children. For example, news accounts of the brutal murder of an eleven-year-old New Jersey boy, Edward Werner, while selling candy door-to-door focused national attention on the tragic cycle of violence among our youth. Fifteen-year-old Sam Manzie has been accused of sexually assaulting and strangling Werner after he rang Manzie's doorbell. The investigation of the crime revealed that Manzi had been involved in a year-long sexual relationship with Stephen Simmons, a forty-three-year-old he met on the Internet. Police described Simmons as a troubled man with a history of preying on children (O'Shaughnessy, 1997).

A few days later, a sixteen-year-old Mississippi boy, Luke Woodham, was accused of stabbing his mother to death with a butcher knife and then driving to school with a rifle and killing two students (including his ex-girlfriend) and wounding several others. "I killed because people like me are mistreated everyday. I did this to show society. Push us, and we'll push back," he stated (O'Shaughnessy, 1997).

Children who are abused or who witness chronic family violence may experience symptoms of posttraumatic stress similar to stress reactions following other types of crises:

- Such physical reactions as enuresis (bedwetting), headaches, sleeping problems, abdominal complaints, and self-abusive behavior
- Changes in eating patterns such as overeating, not eating, and developing eating disorders (a significantly higher rate of eating disorders occurs among female victims of violence; Carll, 1995c)
- Anxiety (the fear that another beating will occur) and depression
- Fear of being separated from the mother, fear of abandonment, and refusal to go to school
- Behavior problems in school

- Higher risks of alcohol/drug abuse and/or juvenile delinquency
- Guilt over not being able to stop the abuse or for loving the abuser

Children who have experienced or witnessed violence at a young age in their families are likely to emulate a pattern of violence in their own homes as adults. Studies estimate that 45 to 80 percent of batterers experienced violence in their homes as children (Buel, 1996; Finkelor, Hotaling, & Yllo, 1988; Sonkin, Martin, & Walker, 1985). The 1994 National Women's Study by Dansk and Brewerton, of the Crime Victims Research and Treatment Center at the Medical University of South Carolina, indicates that 63 percent of the women reported having been raped between the ages of eleven and seventeen. The majority (78 percent) of those women were raped by a relative, boyfriend, or family friend.

Likewise, research has begun to document the relationship between childhood cruelty toward animals/pets and family violence (Arkow, 1992, 1994). In a study of fifty-three families who met the legal criteria for child abuse and neglect, 60 percent also were observed abusing their pets. In 88 percent of homes where physical child abuse occurred, pet abuse also occurred (Deviney, Dickert, & Lockwood, 1983). In retrospective studies of violent criminals and serial killers, cruelty and abuse to animals is frequently noted. Mass murderers Jeffrey Dahmer, Albert DeSalvo, Ted Bundy, David Berkowitz, James Huberty, Carroll Edward Cole, and Earl Shriner all had childhood histories of cruelty and violence to animals (Arkow, 1992, 1994). The recent news report (*Dateline NBC*, October 28, 1997) of Luke Woodham, the sixteen-year-old boy recently accused of killing his mother and shooting, killing, and wounding students at his school, indicated that he had previously tortured and killed his dog. The abuse consisted of pouring lighter fluid down his dog's throat, igniting it, and then drowning the animal.

Cruelty to animals signals a lack of empathy for the suffering of other beings, which may escalate to a lack of empathy for the suffering of humans as well. Parents who abuse their children demonstrate deficits in their capacity for empathy. These abusive behaviors are learned by their children, who, because of the family culture of violence, have not been exposed to prosocial sensitivity and empathy training in the home. This sets the stage for the cycle of abuse to continue into the next generation. The most insidious component of family and community violence is the impact it has on children, who are themselves then implanted with the seeds of violence. Violent behavior is often learned behavior; young children who experience or observe violence as a means of resolving conflict not infrequently go on in later life to employ violence as a conflict-resolving strategy. Obviously a propensity for violence does not begin in adulthood or after one marries; rather, it is a behavior pattern learned at an early age and carried over into teen and adult years.

Although definitive statistics based on large-scale samples of adolescents are unavailable, because this type of data is very difficult to collect, my clinical observation is that there appears to be a dramatic increase in the acceptability of violence as a means of resolving differences in adolescent dating relationships. Anecdotal reports have also been made of an increase in the use of physical force, such as fighting among adolescent females, in the past decade. In schools today, it is not unusual to break up fights between girls; even more telling is the necessity in many schools to search and monitor students of both sexes for weapons.

Violence among the young can also spill over into the community. According to a recent FBI report, violence among youth has increased significantly in the last decade, with 32 percent of all juveniles arrested for crimes being under the age of fifteen. The rise in violence appears to occur among youth as both victims and perpetrators. According to a report published by UNICEF (Howell, 1993), the United States has the highest rate of youth murder in the industrialized world (90 percent of the world's youth murders occur in the United States) As can be seen from the following figures, the industrialized countries listed have significantly lower rates of youth homicides than the United States.

Rate of Homicides per 100,000 Residents
between the Ages of Fifteen and Twenty-Four

United States	15.3
Canada	3.1
Italy	1.9
Norway	1.4
Spain	1.4
Switzerland	1.3
Sweden	1.1
Denmark	1.0
Netherlands	0.9
Britain	0.9
France	0.7
Japan	0.4

RECOMMENDATIONS

To reduce or prevent family violence, we must effect changes in our society, communities, and interpersonal relationships. Effective intervention requires coordinated and collaborative efforts among the legal, judicial, educational, and health care systems, as well as cooperation by the media.

Society and Community Issues

Widespread recognition of the signs of domestic violence and awareness of its baleful impact on individuals and society in general are crucial for change. We must provide training on this topic for health care providers, police officers, lawyers, judges, and even whole school districts. Training should be mandated as continuing education programs and included in the curricula of colleges and universities. Elementary and secondary school districts should provide instruction on recognizing and preventing family violence as part of their health curricula. We must establish simple and accessible procedures by which students can approach faculty or trained peer groups for help. Adolescents often continue in abusive relationships for fear of telling parents. They may be reluctant to "tell" on someone, or they may fear that their parents, in order to protect them, will restrict their activities so drastically as to make their lives intolerable. Parents may be the last to find out about an abusive relationship, which is why it is so important for those in positions of authority to be able to identify abusive situations.

In so many instances, those caught up in a domestic violence situation cannot free themselves by their own efforts alone. They need help, and it is in the best interests of society to see that it is available to them.

Legal and Judicial Issues

Arrest policies should be the same for all violent crimes regardless of whether the victim and offender know each other. This approach would prevent much of the present downplaying of domestic violence and make it more difficult for abusers to pass off incidents as just "family matters." A blow is a blow, and it should not matter if it happened on a street corner between strangers or in a living room between husband and wife. Likewise, sentencing decisions should be based strictly on the nature of the crime and not on the relation of the aggressor to the victim. This measure would serve as a deterrent against domestic battering and sexual violence and, at the least, help get rid of the notion that women and children are property, to be used as the owner wishes. Unfortunately, considerable variability in judicial decisions is apparent now, often with less severe sentencing for assault if the offender happens to be a family member.

The violation of an order of protection should result in the arrest and imprisonment of the offender if it is to serve as a viable deterrent. Because arrest policies vary greatly among jurisdictions, many women do not put much faith in them now. In addition, orders of protection should also require mandatory counseling for the offender.

The development of a computerized system capable of tracking the histories of orders of protection, in all jurisdictions and states, would provide valuable information to a judge when considering issuing an order of protection. For example, a judge could impose a longer time period for the order to be in effect if the offender had a history of multiple orders of protection filed against him or her. In addition, several prior orders of protection would serve as a red flag for potential lethal violence. Take, for example, the young Massachusetts mother, Annie Glenn, who was shot at a school bus stop and died as her two children held her hand and sixteen other children looked on in horror. Her former boyfriend, Richard Kenney, was arrested a few hours later. It turned out that Glenn had two orders of protection against Kenney in 1994, both of which expired well before her death. It was later learned that two other women residing elsewhere in the state had current orders of protection against Kenney (Associated Press, October 22, 1997). Obviously, knowledge of such a violent history would have been valuable in assessing Kenney's dangerousness.

Finally, as stalking in domestic violence cases often escalates to a dangerous situation, stalking must be viewed as a serious crime. The message to the offender has to be clear: stalking will not be tolerated. More stringent antistalking laws are only now beginning to be developed in some parts of the country.

Treatment Interventions for Victims

The treatment of victims must be comprehensive, practical, and focused on the present. Long-term goals can be developed for women who remain in ongoing therapy. The multidimensional treatment approach should include the following components.

Assessment of the Level of Violence and Danger

The following behaviors are indicators of a batterer's potential to cause severe harm, even homicide:

- Threats of homicide and/or suicide
- Severe depression and hopelessness
- Access to weapons
- Alcohol or drug use when depressed or in despair
- Uncontrollable rage
- Obsession with partner
- History of pet and/or animal abuse
- Access to victim and/or family members

Education about Battering

Education should first concentrate on informing the public on how widespread the problem of domestic violence is and how costly it is for society, in terms of resources (police, courts, hospitals) and in irreparably damaged children. It needs to correct the mistaken notions of battering covered in the earlier section on myths, and it must validate the experience of battered women or victims of child abuse and see the plight of these individuals realistically. Such education should also emphasize the cyclical nature of violence and make the public and authorities aware of the difficulties in resolving situations of domestic violence.

Safety Plan

Communities need to plan where a battered woman is to go and what she is to do if she is at risk for violence, including providing information about emergency shelters, restraining orders, and financial issues. If she decides to leave the batterer, a well-thought-out, long-term safety plan is essential to ensure her and her children's safety. Preparation of a go-kit with essential items such as medicine, money, checkbook, car keys, and identification must be made in advance. A woman is at greatest risk for violence and death (Browne, 1987) when she decides to leave. Therefore, a comprehensive safety plan must be in place.

Counseling

The goals in counseling battered women are to develop confidence and empowerment to make changes; to develop independence; to formulate practical plans; to understand the effects of posttraumatic stress; and to understand, grieve, and accept the loss of the relationship. Traditionally, couples experiencing marital difficulties and conflict are seen in conjoint therapy, but couples therapy is inappropriate for cases involving violent individuals. Even if such a couple is attempting to reconcile, conjoint therapy is at best ineffective and at worst dangerous. It is unlikely that a woman will honestly discuss her partner's flaws for fear of retribution when they get home. If she attempts to be honest, her criticism of her partner may trigger an episode of violence and rage at home. Intimidation, present in the home, will not disappear in the therapist's office. The most effective forms of therapy for both victims and batterers entail a combination of individual and group therapy.

Treatment Interventions for Batterers

What is needed is education and emotional support to reinforce egalitarian and nonviolent models of relating, especially in teaching young boys. Focus is also needed on the prevention of developing stereotypes prevalent in adolescence such as that of the "macho" male, who is respected by his peers for acting aggressively and dominating girlfriends. Education must also deal with the question of using violence as a means of control. Counseling for batterers needs to address:

- anger and violence control techniques;
- assertiveness training—how to ask appropriately for what they want;
- stress management—coping with fears;
- conflict resolution;
- communication skills; and
- alcohol and drug abuse.

Community Intervention

Our communities need new public education initiatives to change accepted stereotypes about domestic violence. Such education programs should promote a philosophy of zero tolerance for violence in the home or violence against women and children. Community education should also provide information on how to help someone who is a victim of abuse.

The impact of the increasing depictions of violence in the media has resulted in the perception, particularly in television and film, that violence is entertainment. The deleterious effects of the portrayal of violence against women as well as the impact it has on children contribute to the continued misperceptions and beliefs surrounding domestic and community violence. For public education to be effective, it will require not only massive educational initiatives, public service announcements, information booklets, videos, and news stories but also major changes in the entertainment industry. Accurate portrayal of real-life intimate relationships in movies and television may have far more influence than a barrage of educational campaigns.

Movies and television programming emphasizing prosocial empathetic behavior may prove effective in teaching moral behavior to children. Ongoing efforts to depict socially positive and desirable attributes such as popularity, attractiveness, and strength with prosocial behavior may increase the perceived value of socially desirable behavior and serve as a balance to the emotionally numbing effects of the portrayal of graphic violence against other human beings.

In short, communities and the public at large must recognize the dimensions of the problem of domestic violence and take realistic steps to counter what is now a culture of violence that sees force as an acceptable, even desirable, means of resolving problems. The use of deadly force may at times be necessary in extreme situations, but it is not a social norm and must not be seen as one. The costs of uncontrolled domestic and community violence are just too high for any society to bear.

4

FAMILY VIOLENCE, CUSTODY, AND VISITATION

CHARLES PATRICK EWING, J.D., Ph.D.

Colleen and Dan were married in June 1989 before a large gathering of family and friends. Colleen, then a twenty-two-year-old secretary, had known and dated Dan, a twenty-five-year-old logger, for more than two years. By Colleen's account, their courtship was "wonderful" and Dan was a "perfect gentleman."

A few months later, Colleen gave Dan what she thought was great news: she was pregnant. Although the couple had talked at length and positively about having children, Dan reacted to the news by arguing with Colleen and then punching her in the face and kicking her in the abdomen. The assault was so severe that Colleen had a miscarriage.

After the miscarriage, Dan apologized and begged Colleen to forgive him. He showered her with gifts, flowers, love, and attention. Colleen forgave Dan when he agreed that they would try again to have a child.

Over the next six months, Dan frequently criticized Colleen and was verbally abusive to her, but there was no physical abuse. Six months after her miscarriage, Colleen again became pregnant. The verbal abuse subsided briefly but began anew when Colleen's pregnancy began to show. Dan continually complained that the pregnancy made Colleen look "fat" and "ugly." He ceased showing her any physical affection, and, on two occasions during the pregnancy, Dan struck Colleen in the face with his fist. Colleen confided this abuse to her obstetrician, who referred her to a local battered woman's shelter. Colleen took the shelter's number but never called or sought any other help. Nearly eight months' pregnant, she felt she had no choice but to keep her mouth shut and stay with Dan.

In January 1991, Colleen gave birth to a daughter, Lisa. Dan was present at the child's birth and professed his love for both mother and daughter. For the first few months of Lisa's life, Dan appeared to be a devoted husband and father. Colleen told herself that Dan had finally "grown up" and that the abuse was over. But Colleen was wrong. Before the baby was even six months old, Dan had resumed his abuse of Colleen. Verbal abuse included name-calling ("lazy bitch," "slut," "idiot," "good for nothing," etc.) and constant criticism of Colleen's housekeeping, cooking, and mothering. Dan insisted that Colleen not return to work but refused to allow her access to any money. He demanded that she remain at home, alone with the baby, at all times when he was not there, and he would call her as often as six times a day to make sure she complied.

For the next two years, Colleen put up with this psychological abuse as well as many instances of physical abuse, several of which involved and/or were witnessed by the infant Lisa. Colleen, who became severely depressed, finally sought and received psychotherapy and medication at the county mental health clinic, but she remained in the relationship despite her therapist's urging to the contrary.

On Christmas Day 1993, Dan went on a rampage, trashed the couple's home, and shoved Colleen through a large plateglass storm door. The police were called by a neighbor who witnessed the assault, and Dan was taken into custody under a recently established mandatory arrest policy. The next day, after Dan was released on minimum bail, Colleen obtained a court order of protection and met with an attorney to file for divorce.

Although ordered out of the marital home and told by the criminal court to stay away from both Colleen and Lisa, Dan successfully petitioned the family court to grant him visitation with Lisa every weekend pending the outcome of the divorce litigation. Dan also filed a cross-petition seeking custody of Lisa, claiming that Colleen was an unfit mother by virtue of mental illness. Ultimately, the family court took jurisdiction of the entire case and granted Dan visitation with Lisa. For the next fifteen months, as the divorce and custody cases made their way through the protracted legal process, Dan used the weekly visits with his daughter as a forum for alternately verbally abusing Colleen and pleading with her to take him back. Meanwhile, a psychologist was assigned by the court to evaluate Colleen, Dan, and Lisa, and a law guardian was appointed to represent Lisa's legal interests in the proceedings that would decide her future.

Colleen's victimization and experience with the legal system, though tragic, is far from rare. Every year, hundreds of thousands of American women are abused by the men with whom they share intimate relationships. The abuse varies from relatively minor to extremely severe. Indeed, several hundred women are murdered each year by the men in their lives, and spouse abuse is the leading cause of injury to women in this country.

As Colleen's case illustrates, battering raises concerns about not only the well-being of abused women but also the health, safety, and custody of their children. Even battered women who, like Colleen, manage to find their way out of the battering relationship often find that child custody and visitation laws not only provide their abusers with continued access to them but give the abusers a potent weapon with which to continue abusing them. This chapter examines some of the major legal and clinical issues affecting decision making about custody and visitation issues in families torn apart by domestic violence, and it offers suggestions for mental health and legal professionals charged with making or helping to make these critical decisions.

FAMILY VIOLENCE AND
THE LAW OF CHILD CUSTODY

To fully comprehend the plight of battered women such as Colleen, one needs first to understand the law of child custody and visitation and how the law often works to the detriment of these women and their children.

In earlier times, though often discriminated against by the courts in other ways, battered women were rarely denied custody of their children when they separated from or divorced their batterers. Indeed, not all that long ago in American law, mothers almost always won custody disputes. In fact, few custody disputes actually went to trial because fathers and/or their attorneys were aware of the futility of challenging a mother's claim to custody of her children.

Applying the so-called "tender years doctrine," courts routinely held that young children belonged in the custody of their mothers (Charlow, 1994). And even after that doctrine wore out its welcome in the courtroom, courts continued to favor mothers over fathers on the ground that mothers were generally the children's primary caretakers and more likely to be their "psychological parents" (see Goldstein, Freud, & Solnit, 1973).

Within the past two decades or so, however, the tide has turned. Custody decision-making rules that once favored women have now, all too often, been rejected as gender biased, and courts have begun to look at a broader array of factors in deciding which parent is to be awarded primary custody of a child following divorce. Among the factors that often favor fathers, including many abusers, are greater financial security and the appearance of greater emotional stability.

Additionally, child custody adjudications have been significantly affected in recent years by the trend toward so-called joint custody—a custodial arrangement whereby both parents split the physical and/or legal custody of the child after divorce (see Scott & Derdeyn, 1984). For obvious reasons, the growing preference for joint custody in some jurisdictions has also contributed to a legal climate in which mothers, including battered women, are much less likely to be awarded sole custody of their children following separation or divorce.

Today, whether expressing a preference for joint or sole custody, courts almost invariably adhere to the so-called "best interests of the child" rule in deciding custody and visitation disputes (see Charlow, 1994). And, in so doing, they often look to outside authorities, particularly mental health experts, to evaluate parents and children and help resolve these disputes.

Although some mental health professionals are knowledgeable and experienced in the area of domestic violence, most are not. As a result, in many cases the natural and predictable psychological consequences of battering and the termination of the relationship for the battered woman (e.g., anger, frustration, fear, depression, lack of trust, lack of future plans, etc.) "will be misinterpreted as [evidence of] a pathological disorder that will interfere with her ability to parent her children" (Walker & Edwall, 1987, pp. 141–142).

Even when mental health professionals look to child custody experts for guidance, they may find little help. And, unfortunately, what little help they do find may further contribute to the tendency to stereotype and stigmatize battered women. For example, in one of the best and most recent guides to conducting custody evaluations, *Clinician's Guide to Child Custody Evaluations*, Ackerman (1995) devotes only one page out of approximately three hundred in the book to the issue of spouse abuse. Moreover, virtually all of that space is devoted to a discussion of Veltkamp and Miller's (1990) "spouse abuse accommodation syndrome." Quoting those authors, Ackerman tells child custody evaluators, and those who would assume that role:

The long-term effects of experiencing family violence suggest the following: (1) There tend to be self-destructive tendencies in victims, (2) Women who have been abused show significant adjustment difficulties and problems related to both interpersonal and sexual relationships with males and females, (3) Abuse victims tend to abuse their offspring, thus perpetuating abuse to the next generations. (Ackerman, 1995, p. 167, quoting Veltkamp & Miller, 1990, p. 184)

The adjudication of child custody disputes has also been affected by the emergence of alternative methods of dispute resolution, primarily mediation. In response to the overwhelming load of divorce and custody cases, many courts and attorneys in recent years have expressed a preference for the out-of-court, voluntary settlement of matrimonial and custodial disputes. In turn, this trend has spawned the growing professional field of divorce and custody mediation (see Charlow, 1994; Kelly, Zlatchin, & Shawn, 1985; Walker & Edwall, 1987).

Though the kind of power imbalance virtually inherent in battering relationships has long been recognized as a contraindication to custody mediation (Walker & Edwall, 1987), today many abused women find themselves encouraged and/or required to engage in custody mediation with their abusive partners. Not surprisingly, all too often the result is that abused women feel compelled to compromise in order to avoid further confrontation and abuse, and they end up with custody and visitation arrangements that work to the further detriment of themselves and their children.

Finally, the adjudication of child custody and visitation conflicts has been significantly affected by changing divorce laws. In particular, the move toward no-fault divorce has reduced the relevance of fault in matrimonial proceedings generally, but particularly in those cases involving battered women. As Mahoney (1992) has observed, no-fault laws have made violence against women less visible, moved the relevance of such violence from the divorce proceeding to the custody dispute, and forced battered women to raise the issue defensively in a context in which they, too, are being evaluated and judged.

Cognizant of these and other legal changes, many of which appear to have had adverse effects on battered women seeking to retain custody of their children, the United States Congress, state legislatures, and the courts have recently begun to take steps to ensure that domestic violence is given proper weight in determining what is in any given child's best interests when it comes to custody and visitation.

In 1990, for example, both houses of Congress unanimously passed the following joint resolution:

> Whereas State courts have often failed to recognize the detrimental effects of having as a custodial parent an individual who physically abuses his or her spouse, insofar as the courts do not hear or weigh evidence of domestic violence in child custody litigation;
>
> Whereas there is an alarming bias against battered spouses in contemporary child custody trends such as joint custody and mandatory mediation;
>
> Whereas joint custody guarantees the batterer continued access and control over the battered spouse's life through their children . . .
>
> Whereas a batterer's violence toward an estranged spouse often escalates during or after a divorce, placing both the abused spouse and children at risk through shared custody arrangements and unsupervised visitation;
>
> Whereas physical abuse of a spouse is relevant to child abuse in child custody disputes . . .
>
> Whereas few states have recognized the interrelated nature of child custody and battering and have enacted legislation that allows or requires courts to consider evidence of physical abuse of a spouse in child custody cases . . .
>
> It is the sense of the Congress that, for purposes of determining child custody, credible evidence of physical abuse of a spouse should create a statutory presumption that it is detrimental to the child to be placed in the custody of the abusive spouse. (U.S. House of Representatives, Congressional Resolution 172, 101st Congress, 2nd Session, 1990)

Although Congress has no authority to legislate in the area of child custody decision making, this resolution has not been without impact. In the past several years, many states have heeded

Congress's call for consideration of spouse abuse in child custody and visitation decision making. Today, domestic violence is specified—by statute, case law, or both—as one of a number of child custody decision-making criteria in at least thirty-seven states and the District of Columbia (see Elrod, 1995).

Among the many recent legislative changes in this regard are statutes in Michigan, Vermont, Virginia, Florida, North Dakota, and Missouri. Recent enactments in Michigan, Vermont, and Virginia specify that domestic violence by one parent against the other is a factor to be considered in determining child custody (see Michigan, 1994; Vermont, 1993; Virginia, 1994). A recent Florida statute allows the court to consider a parent's conviction for domestic violence a rebuttable presumption against shared parenting of a child (Florida, 1994). Similarly, a North Dakota law creates a rebuttable presumption against the award of sole or joint custody to a parent determined by credible evidence to have perpetrated domestic violence (North Dakota, 1993).

Finally, in yet another example of lawmaking on this subject, the Missouri legislature has enacted a law requiring that custody shall be awarded in order to protect the child and any other family members who have been the victims of family violence and that when custody is awarded to an abusive parent, the court must justify the decision with specific findings (Missouri, 1994).

FAMILY VIOLENCE AND THE LAW OF VISITATION

The relationship between parent and child is so fundamental that courts have routinely held that even when a parent is denied physical custody of a child, absent exceptional circumstances, the noncustodial parent has an inviolable right to visitation with the child. Indeed, only under the most extraordinary circumstances will a biological parent be cut off from all contact with his or her child (Haralambie, 1993). For example, courts have even gone so far as to require visitation between a child and father in cases in which the father has been convicted of and incarcerated for an act of criminal violence against the child's mother (e.g., *Lewis v. Lewis,* 1994).

Typically, when one parent is awarded primary custody of a child, the noncustodial parent is granted what the law calls visitation, parent access, or parent–child contact. For example, when a mother is granted primary physical custody, the child will reside with her but have contact with the father on a regularly scheduled and enforceable basis. A typical visitation schedule might include one evening during the week and an overnight visit every other weekend.

Additionally, visitation orders may allow for contacts between noncustodial parent and child during school vacations and holidays and also provide for telephone contacts at other times. Some court orders go so far as to spell out specific holidays, vacation periods, and even the time, day of the week, and duration of telephone calls.

Demands for visitation are routinely made and routinely granted. Indeed, visitation is regarded as so important that, in some states, courts are required to consider parental cooperation in visitation as a factor in deciding custody. For example, when a court finds that a mother is unlikely to allow frequent and continuing contact between father and child, that factor may be viewed as inconsistent with the child's best interests, the court may infer that the mother is an unfit parent, and custody may be awarded to the father. Moreover, when parental interference with visitation occurs after custody has been awarded, such interference or lack of cooperation with visitation might be regarded as grounds for changing custody (i.e., awarding custody to the parent whose visitation with the child has been hindered; see Haralambie, 1993).

Even when a court does not take the drastic step of changing custody, interference with visitation may lead to other sanctions against the custodial parent (see Haralambie, 1993). The interfering parent may be held in contempt of court, fined, required to pay the other parent's attorney's fees, or even be jailed if the interference is found to be willful. In some states, willful interference with visitation is a crime.

The importance courts and legislatures have attached to visitation between child and noncustodial parent is understandable. In our society, the right to bear and raise children is regarded as fundamental, both philosophically and legally. Ideally, a child should grow up with a relationship to both of his or her parents. But, when one parent is a perpetrator of domestic violence who has abused the other parent and/or the child, there may be a need to limit or curtail the child's relationship with the abusive parent.

In recent years, courts and legislatures have begun to consider domestic violence not only as a factor in awarding custody but also as a criterion in decision making about visitation. Clearly, when a child has been physically or sexually abused by a parent, courts can and routinely do shape visitation orders to protect the abused child. Such orders often deny and/or seriously limit the visitation between abusive parent and abused child (see Ackerman, 1995).

Maryland law, for example, provides that "unless the court specifically finds that there is no likelihood of further child abuse or neglect by the party, the court shall deny custody or visitation rights to that party, except that the court may approve a supervised visitation arrangement that assures the safety and the physiological, psychological, and emotional well-being of the child" (Haralambie, 1993, p. 314).

But when a child has not been physically or sexually abused by a parent, many courts now have the explicit authority to deny or limit visitation between the child and parent if they find that a parent has been the perpetrator of domestic violence. Typically, such cases arise when one parent, usually the father, has not directly abused the child but has been physically abusive to the other parent, usually the mother.

In Arizona, for instance, when the court finds evidence of domestic violence, it must arrange visitation in a manner that best protects the child and the abused parent from further harm. Moreover, the law in that state places on the abusive parent the burden of proving to the court that visitation will not seriously endanger the child's welfare (Arizona, 1993). Similar laws are now on the books in numerous other states. For example, in California, Hawaii, Maryland, Montana, Virginia, Washington, and Wisconsin, among other jurisdictions, courts are now required to consider evidence of domestic violence in making determinations about the feasibility, nature, and limitation of visitation between child and perpetrating parent (see Haralambie, 1993, p. 315, n. 66).

Some states have gone even further in their efforts to protect children from parents who engage in domestic violence. In Oklahoma, for example, proof of ongoing domestic violence by clear and convincing evidence establishes a rebuttable presumption that it is not in a child's best interests to have unsupervised visitation with the parent who is the perpetrator of such violence (Oklahoma, 1990).

DOMESTIC VIOLENCE, CUSTODY AND VISITATION: THE LAW IN ACTION

As is the case in virtually all areas of the law, child custody and visitation law on the books is one thing; the law in practice is another. Though recent enactments, such as those described earlier, should make it easier for battered women to protect themselves and their children from their batterers, application of these laws remains inconsistent and subject to many limitations, both legal and practical.

Legal Limitations

Perhaps the most significant legal limitations battered women still face when seeking custody and visitation rulings that protect them and their children are those caused by the slow pace at which the courts work and the lack of finality of their judgments.

Consider the case of Jill, a hypothetical mother of two children, who, after years of abuse by her husband, Jack, has finally been able to bring herself to file for divorce. When Jill consults an attorney, she learns several things that dampen her enthusiasm for divorce.

First, Jill learns that unless Jack is willing to cooperate and not contest the divorce, she will have to prove that she has grounds for divorce. She also learns that if Jack does contest the divorce, the ensuing litigation could take years, and that even if he does not contest the divorce, the proceedings will certainly take many months to complete.

Even more significantly, Jill learns that except in the most unusual circumstances (e.g., when there is a proven and substantial physical threat to the woman or her children), courts are generally unwilling to force an abuser to leave the marital home permanently. Thus, Jill discovers that while the case makes its way through the court system, she and her children may be forced to remain living in the same home with the man who has abused her.

Jill's attorney, in fact, is likely to advise her not to move out of the marital home because doing so might later be held against her in the divorce, custody, and/or visitation proceedings. The attorney is also likely to advise Jill not to remove the children from the home without consent from the court and/or Jack, because to do so might work to her prejudice when the court has to decide temporary and/or permanent custody.

Even a battered woman who has simply moved in with family or friends or taken up residence in a shelter may find herself charged with custodial interference or even kidnapping if she removes her children from the home without such permission.

Additionally, Jill will undoubtedly learn from her attorney that even if she and Jack do separate pending divorce, there is no certainty that she will be awarded temporary custody of the children, since temporary custody decisions are often made without a full consideration of all the facts. Moreover, Jill's attorney will probably warn her that the court's temporary custody decision often proves to be crucial because, given the protracted nature of legal proceedings, the temporary order may be in effect for so long that it will be difficult if not impossible to change it when the court finally gets around to making a final order.

Jill's lawyer will also likely advise her that even if she obtains temporary custody, pending the outcome of the proceedings, Jack will almost certainly be given liberal visitation, at least pending a full judicial hearing on the matter, which may take many months to schedule and complete.

Jill will also learn that in the event custody and/or visitation issues are litigated, she, Jack, and the children can expect to run a lengthy gauntlet of mental health and child custody evaluation sessions, in-home visits and assessments, and interviews with one or more law guardians—all of which will take time and contribute to delay in an already protracted proceeding.

Jill may also learn that when it comes to custody evaluations, if either she or Jack is not satisfied with the evaluator's conclusions, he or she may ask the court to allow another expert to conduct an additional evaluation. In fact, she may learn that in some cases, as many as three such evaluations end up being done—one by appointment of the court, one by the father's chosen expert, and one by the mother's.

Finally, Jill will almost certainly learn from her attorney that when it comes to child custody and visitation decisions, "even when it's over, it's not over." A candid attorney will tell Jill that all child custody and visitation decisions are temporary in the sense that they can be (and often are) challenged legally, relitigated and altered any time one of the parents raises a claim of substantially changed circumstances. This point means, for example, that even if Jill divorces her husband and secures custody of her two young children, Jack may continue to battle her legally for custody and/or increased visitation should circumstances change significantly (e.g., if either parent remarries, wishes to relocate, or claims that a change in the child's needs warrants a change in custody or visitation).

Practical Limitations

Even when battered women are able to surmount these legal limitations, they may still be unable to obtain justice for themselves and their children because of practical limitations.

Money, or more precisely the lack thereof, is undoubtedly the most significant practical barrier battered women face when they seek custody of their children and/or try to limit their abuser's visitation. To begin with, in many if not most battering relationships, batterers control the finances. Thus, even in financially secure families, an abused woman may have limited or no access to funds needed to obtain legal counsel and to litigate child custody and visitation disputes.

In families without financial resources, neither party may have the ability to obtain counsel to litigate these issues, and the couple may be forced to negotiate a settlement—one that, given the dynamics of abusive relationships, will in all likelihood favor the abuser at the expense of the battered woman and their children.

Beyond money, however, success in any kind of litigation often requires tenacity, stamina, and perseverance. As a result of their abuse victimization, battered women often suffer from depression, hopelessness, and other psychological problems that limit their ability to take and maintain a strong legal position against their abusers. Unfortunately, without tremendous social support and good professional help, many battered women will simply be psychologically unable to endure the adversary rigors of protracted, often ugly court battles over custody and visitation.

On the other hand, their batterers frequently show a remarkable ability to persist in litigation and to use it as a form of continued abuse. Indeed, a good deal of custody and visitation litigation initiated by abusive men appears to be little more than an effort to assert continued control and dominance over "their" women.

SOME SUGGESTIONS FOR LEGAL AND MENTAL HEALTH PROFESSIONALS

Although researchers, the media, and other sources of public information have shattered many of the myths about battered women and battering relationships, many still believe that disso-lution of the battering relationship brings about an end to batter-ing. As detailed earlier, that belief often proves to be false. Indeed, in some cases, the worst abuse occurs when the woman decides to take necessary and appropriate steps to terminate the relationship.

Thus, when dealing with child custody and visitation issues, legal and mental health professionals must keep in mind that when abuse has occurred, there is a strong likelihood that abuse may continue, even though abuser and victim are now living apart. To put it more directly, there is every reason to believe that battered women and their children remain at risk for abuse even after separation or divorce.

A related concern is the identification of families who have experienced domestic violence. Despite a lack of systematic data, it seems fair to say that a substantial percentage of custody and visitation disputes involve families in which domestic violence of one sort or another has taken place. Some authorities have esti-mated that more than half the families involved in custody dis-putes have a history of domestic violence (see, e.g., Walker & Edwall, 1987).

In some instances, these families will be self-identified—that is, the woman and/or children will reveal the abuse in legal pleadings or in the course of custody evaluations. Often, how-ever, the same dynamics that may have kept abuse a family secret prior to separation and divorce will continue to operate even af-ter the legal processes have been initiated. As a result, legal and mental health professionals must treat every custody and visita-tion dispute as though it might involve a history of domestic vio-lence. Lawyers, law guardians, judges and mental health experts should carefully assess and review each such case for evidence of spouse and/or child abuse. In many if not most instances, this consideration will mean directly asking the parties and their chil-dren about abuse within the family.

Recognition of the problem, though obviously a necessary first step, is not sufficient. Legal and mental health professionals must be aware of the dynamics of battering relationships so that they do not stereotype and make false assumptions about abused women, their role in the abusive relationship, and their parenting capacities. Lawyers, judges, evaluators, and all others who play a role in deciding custody and visitation issues need education and training with regard to domestic violence and its impact on families and children, both before and after divorce or separation.

Lawyers, law guardians, and especially judges need not only to become educated about family violence but also to utilize what they learn. In all too many instances, courts fail to give child custody and visitation cases the high priority and serious attention they deserve. Cases are sometimes allowed to drag on for months, even years, without resolution; judicial pressure is placed on the parties to mediate and/or settle; and when the court is forced to make a decision, judges often look to the law and/or the experts for a simple solution. To allow this outcome to happen in any case is reprehensible, but to do so in cases in which children and their mothers are at risk for continued abuse is inexcusable.

Though obviously constrained by law, no judge in any jurisdiction is required to decide a custody or visitation case on any basis contrary to the child's best interests. Judges and other legal professionals involved in custody and visitation litigation must recognize, first and foremost, what the laws in some states are just beginning to tell them: *It is presumptively contrary to the best interests of any child to place that child in the custody of, or to allow unsupervised visitation with, a parent who has abused the child or the child's other parent.*

In any case in which abuse is alleged or even suspected, courts should proceed with extreme caution, granting any kind of custody (sole or even joint) to an abusive parent only in the most unusual circumstances (i.e., when no viable alternative exists and the court can be assured that the child's safety and psychological well-being will not be compromised).

Courts should exercise similar caution in granting visitation to abusive parents. Although the law makes it difficult, if not almost impossible, to cut off all contact between an abusive parent and his child(ren), courts invariably have the authority to fashion visitation arrangements capable of protecting the child and his or her mother. For example, courts may order that all visitation be supervised and/or arranged in such a way as to prevent contact between the abusive parent and the abused parent.

Finally, judges, law guardians, and lawyers need to be reminded that custody and visitation cases ought to be resolved with the utmost dispatch. Delay in these cases—whether in holding hearings or rendering a decision—hurts all parties to such litigation, but especially battered women and their children whose physical and psychological well-being remain at risk every day the legal system postpones action.

Though not the ultimate decision makers in child custody and visitation cases, mental health experts often play a crucial if not determinative role, especially in cases in which there is evidence of domestic violence. Unfortunately, these professionals, like their legal counterparts, sometimes make matters worse.

In conducting all custody and visitation evaluations, mental health professionals must not only be alert to but actually look for evidence of domestic violence. All persons interviewed, including parents, children, and significant others, should be appropriately queried regarding abuse within the family.

When allegations of domestic violence emerge prior to or during the course of the evaluation, they should be thoroughly investigated, and the evaluation should be given the highest priority for prompt completion.

When the evaluator has reason to believe or suspect that a child is at risk, either physically or emotionally, he or she should take immediate steps to minimize or remove that risk. When appropriate, evaluators should, of course, comply with mandated child abuse reporting laws (see Levine & Doueck, 1995). But even when there is no evidence or reasonable suspicion of *current* abuse, evaluators should carefully consider making an immediate, interim report to the court.

In making that determination, it is crucial that evaluators have ready access to the lawyers, the law guardian, if any, and the judge. Evaluators should never assume that the court is aware of information simply because others are.

Custody and visitation evaluators must also strive to avoid the kinds of myths, stereotypes, and sexist biases that sometimes lead them to underestimate a battered woman's parenting capacity and/or the continuing threat posed to her and her children by her abusive spouse. At a minimum, evaluators should take great care to avoid misinterpreting the predictable effects of abuse victimization as evidence of pathology or inadequate parenting.

5

STALKING IN THE COMMUNITY AND WORKPLACE

DAVID M. BATZA AND MICHELLE TAYLOR

In 1975, Angie Jones (not her real name) married Robert when she was only fourteen years old. Robert developed a serious substance abuse problem, which included his regularly abusing alcohol, cocaine, and crack. He also developed a pattern of physical abuse and controlling behavior. He once sat on the couch next to Angie, put his hands around her neck, and explained that she was only alive because he wanted her alive.

Robert was diagnosed as a diabetic. He required everyone in his family to stick to his required diet. Robert made it Angie's responsibility to make him take his insulin as proof that she loved him.

Robert developed delusional thoughts, including his belief that the Drug Enforcement Administration planted bugs in his house and car.

Robert once asked his daughter's friends to leave his house and began firing a shotgun at them because they did not leave fast enough. He also fired a shotgun at his friends in a similar situation. After spending seven days locked in a garage doing drugs with his friends, Robert decided it was time for them to leave, so he began firing his shotgun at them.

Angie left Robert on several occasions, staying away for a short period and then returning home. On July 3, 1994, Angie again left Robert, moved in with her sister, filed for a divorce, and obtained a temporary restraining order (TRO).

Robert threatened to kill Angie's friends and family members for helping Angie leave. Angie's sister maintained contact with Robert on a regular basis, in an attempt to dissuade his inappropriate behavior.

Robert's brother notified Angie's friends and family of Robert's death threats. He also stated his fear for his safety and advised that Robert's entire family was afraid of him. Robert was contacted by police on at least three occasions and warned to stop his inappropriate behavior.

Robert learned that Angie was dating another man. He called every telephone number on their telephone bills in an effort to determine who and where this man was.

On July 24, 1994, Robert called Angie and said, "The only promise I promise to keep is to take out everyone in that house. I'm a lot closer than you think, and if you don't believe me, step out your door." He then admitted he did not mind going to jail and that if he did go to jail, he would get out eventually. He then stated, "I want you to hear something." Angie heard the sound of a shotgun shell being jacked into a chamber. Robert said, "You know what I have, and you know what I can do."

Robert reported that he and his daughter went looking for Angie every night. He made every effort to meet with Angie before their divorce court date. Sometimes he said he wanted to find her to get back together with her, and other times he said he found a buyer for their house and needed her to sign release papers.

At this point, this case was most similar to those situations that escalate to the point of posing hazard. In fact, on a scale of 1 to 10, this case was a 10. Angie's employer did many things to create a safe work environment, including transferring Angie to another location, implementing additional security measures to prevent Robert from entering the work environment, and setting up a voice mail system to capture his calls. In fact, he called several times in an attempt to get information about Angie, and he visited once but was stopped by security.

Acting against expert advice, Angie, her family, and her friends did not stop contact with Robert, as they should have. Angie did not make herself unavailable to him, rejecting the suggestion that she move and establish a new residence in such a way that would prevent Robert from finding her. Despite her fear, Angie was reluctant to make changes in her life to improve her personal safety. She felt that moving was too great an inconvenience, and she was not going to be "pushed around" by her husband anymore.

On September 23, 1994, Robert located Angie's car outside her sister's residence. He broke into their home with a shotgun and a machete. He believed he saw Angie through the sliding-glass door trying to escape and fired his shotgun. He missed. A boyfriend came out of a bedroom and shot and killed Robert.

This case certainly could have ended tragically with Angie dead on her sister's floor. Last-minute intervention by another saved her life. But the whole situation could have been avoided if Angie had taken a few preventive measures.

There are two sides to any assessment of stalking. To ignore the victim's accessibility and vulnerability to an unwanted encounter with a stalker would be like assessing the risks of skydiving by considering only the hardness of the ground and ignoring the operation of the parachute. The advantages that are in place or available to reduce the likelihood of an encounter must be considered.

Some victims of stalking, such as Angie Jones, believe it is simpler to modify the behavior of the stalker rather than their own, but this view rarely proves to be accurate. Accordingly, in the assessment and management of stalking cases, elements of the situations surrounding both the victim and the stalker must be considered.

This chapter will discuss the assessment of stalking situations, their management, and preventive measures that can reduce the likelihood of becoming a victim. The underlying and most important message, however, is that stalking cases are predictable, preventable, and manageable.

CATEGORIES OF CASES

Every stalking case contains a unique set of factors specific to that case. There are, however, common characteristics of stalkers and common behavioral patterns in stalking situations that enable the identification of categories and specific factors relevant to those categories. This chapter will focus on public figure stalking and interpersonal stalking.

Public figure stalking involves any public figure who is being stalked by a member of the general public. *Interpersonal stalking* describes any situation in which a person is being stalked by a person with whom he or she has had a relationship, such as a coworker, acquaintance, friend, boyfriend, girlfriend, or spouse.

Both public figure and interpersonal stalkers can be categorized by one of four main types of motivation: attachment seekers, identity seekers, rejection-based stalkers, and delusion-based stalkers. *Attachment seekers* pursue in order to obtain some type of relationship—for example, marriage or a business relationship. *Identity seekers* pursue in order to obtain some identity—for example, a doctor's wife or an assassin. *Rejection-based stalkers* pursue in order to reverse, correct, or avenge a rejection—for example, a termination or a divorce. *Delusion-based stalkers* pursue in response to their delusions—for example, the belief that a public figure is his or her spouse.

Stalkers may have a mixture of these motives. For example, attachment seekers who select a famous person as a romantic object and say they want a relationship might also be seeking the identity of a movie star's wife. Stalkers might be pursuing a relationship in response to some delusion.

Rejection-based stalkers and identity seekers are most likely to pursue hazardous action against their victim. Attachment seekers rarely attack unless they are first moved into the category of rejection-based, where few cases start.

ASSESSMENT

The question to answer when assessing a stalking case is, What is the likelihood that a particular case will escalate to the point of posing hazard to the victim? The first—and natural—question usually asked by the victim is, Is he dangerous? Unfortunately, that is a difficult, if not impossible, question to answer because dangerousness is situational. Dangerousness is not a permanent state of being or an attribute of a person. For a situation to be dangerous, there must be sinister intent (or at least disregard for another's safety), there must be the means to deliver harm, there must be a victim who is vulnerable and accessible, and there must be a set of circumstances that provide advantage to the attacker.

The term *potentially dangerous* should also be avoided because most people can be provoked to the point that they act dangerously under certain circumstances. For example, if a person held a loaded gun to the head of someone you love, you would likely, and appropriately, act in a dangerous manner toward that person if doing so would save your loved one. Accordingly, in assessing a stalking situation, all relevant factors are determined in an effort to predict the likelihood that a stalker will escalate his pursuit to the point of posing hazard to the victim.

The factors to assess include past and present information about the stalker, the history of the case, including all communications, and measures that would make it less likely that a stalker would succeed at posing hazard to a particular victim.

The computer assessment program designed by Gavin de Becker, called MOSAIC™, measures these factors. To determine whether a situation is likely to escalate to the point of posing hazard to the victim, the important characteristics of the case are identified, coded, and entered into MOSAIC™, which instantly compares those characteristics with thousands of other cases.

These conclusions cannot, in themselves, guide a management plan because each case is unique. Still, the information provides a foundation on which to base certain assumptions.

The specific factors vary depending on the type of case being assessed. In a public figure case, the following factors are considered:

- Motivational category
- Content, emotional tone, and clarity of the communications
- Intensity of efforts to communicate
- Method of communicating
- Indicators of urgency
- Accreditation
- How the stalker projected himself
- How the stalker projected the public figure
- Stalking conduct
- Familiarity with the target environment
- Similarity to past attackers
- Age
- History of police encounters
- Residency
- Employment
- Mental health history
- Weapons possession, access, or interest
- Neighbor relations
- Location
- Financial situation
- Travel history
- History of contact with other public figures
- Other factors that may be unique to the situation

One of the most common misconceptions in the assessment of public figure stalking is the alarm caused by death threats. No known modern-age public figure attacker threatened to kill his or her victim prior to doing so. This does not, however, hold true in other types of stalking situations in which threats are important predictors of future violence.

In an interpersonal stalking case more information is available for assessment than is generally available in most other kinds of cases. The victim usually has intimate knowledge about the stalker's history, his day-to-day activities, and how he interacts with others.

In an interpersonal stalking case, the following factors are considered:

- The pace at which the relationship developed
- Expectations of the relationship
- How the relationship ended, including his reactions
- Ability to accept rejections
- Motivational category
- Interventions
- Negotiations
- Identity tied to the relationship
- Financial situation
- Social situation
- Residential situation
- Adverse contact with law enforcement
- How the stalker resolves conflict
- Enlistment of significant others
- Jealousy
- Projection of emotions
- Use of threats, intimidation, or manipulations
- Use of surveillance
- Control
- Stalking
- Age
- Neighbor relations
- Flexibility
- Interest in or identification with themes of power and violence
- Substance abuse
- Possession, access, or interest in weapons
- Temperament
- Persecutory thoughts and feelings
- Inflexibility

- Identification or comparison with violent people
- Mood swings
- Anger
- Depression
- Blaming others
- Weapons as a substantial part of his persona
- Worldview
- Self-worth
- Significant childhood events
- Victim fear

When the interpersonal stalking case involves domestic violence, in addition to the previously listed factors, the following factors are also considered:

- The victim's intuitive feelings about her risk
- The use of symbolic violence such as breaking things with sentimental value
- Prior history of battering
- Extreme and frequent violence
- Monetary control
- Minimization of incidents of abuse
- Use of "male privilege"
- Experienced or witnessed violence as a child
- Whether the victim made plans to be carried out in the event of her death

When the interpersonal stalking case involves a coworker in the workplace, in addition to the prior factors, the following factors are also considered:

- Allusions to violence against others in the company
- Inappropriate communications to coworkers or supervisors
- Documentation or research of coworkers
- Paranoia
- Repeated accusations of other people causing one's problems

- Refusal to accept termination
- One-sided contact with coworkers following termination
- Litigiousness or unreasonable grievances

These factors do not occur just in isolation—they occur in patterns. Each new case begins to sound familiar because it is the same patterns again and again. There are not always the same combination of factors, and almost never are all factors present. These factors are measured along a continuum and in various combinations when assessing the likelihood of escalation or violence between the stalker and the victim.

The factor most frequently asked about by potential victims is criminal history. People want to know whether their stalker has ever been convicted of a crime, especially a violent or behavioral crime. Although this information is important because the probability of future crime is thought to increase with each prior criminal act, it is only one factor to be considered. A history of violence may demonstrate how that person deals with aggression or conflict. For that reason, a history of violent behavior is relevant to an assessment, but the absence of violent behavior might be irrelevant to the assessment.

Another very important aspect to assessing stalking cases are inhibitors. *Inhibitors* are factors in a person's life that lessen the likelihood of violence such as family or support system, home, career, self-esteem, freedom, dignity, financial situation, living situation, pending legal or criminal action, hobbies, and interests. When inhibitors are not present or dominant and one is sufficiently provoked, violence becomes quite possible.

For most people, the things that could be lost as a result of committing violence serve as inhibitors against that violence. People rarely act out violently unless they have little else to lose. Therefore, when assessing a serious stalking case, it is important to conduct an investigation of the stalker to determine the level of inhibitors.

If a stalker has a loving wife and family, a good financial situation, a positive outlook, and plenty of options, he represents less of a safety concern. A recently divorced stalker who lost custody of his children, is about to lose his home, had his car repossessed, and whose mother just passed away is more of a safety concern.

The intuition of the victim and those familiar with the case should also be considered. Intuition is a complex thought process that recognizes signals people may not even consciously know are signals. Unfortunately, people in our culture are very reluctant to listen to intuition. The history of violent crime is full of evidence that people felt uncomfortable, threatened, intimidated, or unsafe because of the very person who later committed an act of violence against them. Many people consider intuition an emotional or unreasonable process. Those people generally prefer a logical, explainable, unemotional thought process from which they can find a supportable conclusion.

Intuition is often expressed in humor. Humor, especially dark humor, is a common way for people to communicate true concern without the risk of feeling silly afterwards and without overtly showing fear. The following is a true story of how Bob Taylor's intuition was expressed in his humor:

Bob Taylor works at the California Forestry Association. One day the receptionist was out, so Taylor and others at his office sorted the mail. They came across an unusual package. They looked it over and talked about what to do with it. It was addressed to the former president of the association, and they considered forwarding it to him. When Gilbert Murray, the current president arrived, they brought him into their discussion. Murray said, "Let's open it." Taylor, however, got up and cracked a joke: "I'm going back to my office before the bomb goes off." As he walked down the hall to his desk, he heard the enormous explosion that killed his boss.

That package was sent by the Unabomber. It was very heavy for its size, covered with tape, had too much postage, and aroused enough interest that morning that several people speculated on whether it might be a bomb. Still, it was opened. They had noted the Oakland firm named on the return address, and if they had called Directory Assistance, they would have found it was not a listed company.

The moral of the story is that it is also important to consider intuition when assessing a case.

MANAGEMENT STRATEGIES

Many management responses are possible in situations involving stalking. Not all are necessarily applicable, practical, or appropriate for every case, and some carry the risk of worsening the situation.

Several management strategies fall into the category of interventions—for example, enlisting the help of the stalker's parents or relatives, pursuing a temporary restraining order (TRO) or an injunction against harassment, giving a prewarning for trespassing, participating in police interviews, responding to or returning unopened communications, prosecuting for postal service violations, pursuing a court-ordered peace bond or protection order, and following through with criminal prosecution.

Other commonly applied management strategies include surveillance, protective coverage, and monitoring. An effective management strategy should also always include attention to preventive measures, such as making the residence address undiscoverable to those who may seek to find it and implementing security measures.

Some of these management strategies will be effective with a particular case, and some will not. Some will enhance safety, and others will detract from safety. In fact, any of these, a combination of these, or none of these might be the best management plan for a given case. There is no one answer to stalking cases.

Interventions

Whether or not to apply interventions to stalkers is one of the most complicated and challenging questions in managing a stalking case. Many types of intervention are possible, but this section will focus on direct interventions, which are intended to force or convince a stalker to stop his pursuit. A common intervention involves meeting with the stalker and advising him that the object of his pursuit does not want any contact or any relationship with him. Variations of this approach include warning him that he would be arrested or the subject of legal action, warning him about unspecified harms that might befall him if he continues his pursuit, urging, cajoling, or otherwise trying to induce a person to stop. Arrest is an intervention, as is the obtaining of a TRO (and subsequent injunction against harassment).

In public figure stalking, successful encounters in which stalkers act with lethal force are rare. Successful encounters in which stalkers did not act out dangerously are also uncommon, given the number of people who have sought or are seeking such encounters. We are left then to study those who attacked, the only population who can inform us about attackers as opposed to stalkers. The far smaller population of attackers includes several cases in which direct interventions were applied prior to the attacks.

Intervention opportunities only exist among those cases that are recognized prior to their attacks. In other words, if someone shows up and conducts an attack without offering any detectable preincident indicator, thus providing no opportunity to apply intervention or to decide not to apply intervention, then such a case could not be relevant to the intervention question—there would be no opportunity to ask it. Fortunately, such cases are extremely rare; nearly every public figure attacker in the media age provided some detectable preincident indicator.

Sirhan Sirhan, who assassinated Robert Kennedy in 1968, exemplifies a public figure attacker who did not provide detectable preincident indicators, and, unfortunately, presidential candidates did not receive Secret Service protection at that time. The efficient logistical support, advance work, and on-the-scene intervention that the Secret Service provides for protectees would likely have foiled that attack.

Of cases in which people did act out dangerously, in some cases intervention was applied and the people still acted (Sara Jane Moore, Samuel Byck, Robert Bardo, Arthur Jackson, Edward

Taylor are examples), and in some cases no intervention was applied, and they still acted. The group of possible attackers who might draw our attention includes an overwhelming majority who would not act violently regardless of intervention, some who would decide not to act because of intervention, some who would decide to act because of intervention, and some who would act out violently in either situation.

The motivational category is an important factor to consider before applying intervention. Rejection-based stalkers are generally bad candidates for intervention because intervention is more rejection. Many interventions humiliate these stalkers by re-expressing the rejection. They are doing what they do because they cannot accept what they perceive as rejection, which generally makes intervention unsuccessful with rejection-based stalkers.

Attachment seekers are viable candidates for intervention, particularly Secret Service–type intervention (direct in-person interviews by agents), because that delivers some attachment (albeit to agents). Still, we must be careful not to move them into rejection-based stalkers. (Bardo may have appeared to be an attachment seeker, but he was actually an identity seeker moved to a rejection-based stalker; Hinckley was an identity seeker; Taylor was an attachment seeker who was moved to rejection-based stalker.)

Identity seekers are also viable candidates for Secret Service–type intervention, because the attention they get somewhat soothes their need. Also, attachment and identity seekers are likely to transfer targets. They often transfer targets to another person who is an instrument that can bring them identity.

Rejection-based stalkers are not as likely to transfer targets. They are focused on the person or people they feel rejected them. Victims or their representatives who continually restate the rejection, perhaps feeling that one version will be more palatable than another, are facilitating the stalker's continued emotional investment. Victims and their representatives who escalate the intensity of rejections (TROs, police warnings, etc.) are taking a rejection that was intolerable when private and making it public.

Delusion-based stalkers can also be moved into other categories by intervention, though intervention may carry less risk here. The nature of delusions is that they are unshakable even in the face of strong evidence. Therefore, the intervention will not likely affect the delusion. There is still the risk of moving them to a rejection-based stalker.

An instructive comparison for a rejection-based stalker is that of an angry former employee. He will not likely be made better by extended discussions of the firing, the controversies that led there, or the company's escalating desire to have nothing to do with him.

It is also important to consider the likelihood that stalkers have already had plenty of intervention prior to an assessment. Attachment seekers, delusion-based stalkers, and most identity seekers have usually had many interventions applied by their families throughout their lives. Urgings, pleadings, warnings, and other efforts to change the stalker's inappropriate behavior have likely been attempted by family or friends. Even some rejection-based stalkers have already been subjected to efforts to change their minds or get them to let go of the issues that consume them. But, alas, as demonstrated by the fact that stalkers in all categories kept up their pursuit, straight talk usually does not work with unreasonable people.

Another important consideration is when in the evolution of a case should intervention be applied. There is always a threshold behavior that triggers intervention, though that threshold may vary. Often, given no detectable response, public figure stalkers will turn their attention elsewhere.

Many stalking cases that continue for years involve perceived "wars" between the stalker and victim. They became emotional campaigns, as opposed to the thousands of pursuits that became boring to the stalker, so he stopped or, more often, turned his attention elsewhere. Even in cases of highly motivated stalkers, public figure targets often need only avoid an encounter or two before the stalker turns his attention elsewhere. This, of course, only applies if there are no interactions that fuel the fire or reenergize the pursuit.

A different dynamic applies for public figures who are provided official protection. Here, the persons who might show up to interview a threatener may be perceived more as representatives of the state or the nation than as representatives of the individual. In these cases, substantial improvement is often noted after intervention, particularly in those cases that are focused on an issue as opposed to an individual.

The following is a common situation: A mentally ill man sends disturbing letters to a female media figure who becomes concerned that he might pose a threat to her safety. He has signed his letters with his true name and provided his address. The media figure knows a private detective who tells her she must do something and says he can intervene and solve the problem: "Just leave it to me."

The detective visits the letter writer at his home and applies an intimidation: "She doesn't want to know you; if she wanted to speak with you, she'd have answered your letters. Don't write to her again. You can get into lots of trouble if you send another letter; I'd hate to have to bring charges on this." The man sends a few more letters and then seems to disappear. He does not pursue harmful actions. The media figure and the detective are pleased with the success of the intervention strategy that combines reason and logic.

The "success" in this story is measured by the fact that, following the intervention, the man did not pursue harmful actions toward the media figure. This assessment fails to recognize that the letter writer might not have had the characteristics likely to produce a dangerous situation in any event. If a person never intends to act dangerously, then almost any intervention might be perceived as a success.

The problem arises when an encounter involves someone who actually is likely to act dangerously. Then, the interventions applied become a serious matter, perhaps the difference between life and death. Statistically, so few people actually carry out attacks against public figures that it is relatively "safe" to apply interventions; odds are the stalker will not act violently after the intervention. The odds are also that the stalker would not have acted before the intervention or in the absence of the intervention. But it is not a game of odds—it is a matter of safety.

On the other end of the scale, intervention like the one described earlier, when applied to situations that have the ingredients of danger, may well worsen and provoke the stalker. It amounts to a form of Russian roulette: one bullet is loaded in a gun with six chambers, and the player spins the cylinder before pulling the trigger. Even though the odds are good, six to one in the person's favor, no reasonable person wants to play.

Police interventions intended to change a stalker's mind or put a cost on his conduct are best applied when a stalker has committed a crime. They should be swift and effective, with the aim to arrest and charge the stalker, not to chat. When police warn someone and then they leave without arrest, they hope to deter but may get the opposite result. As the officers leave, the stalker just faced the single greatest weapon in the victim's arsenal: the police. They talked to him and he survived without any impact on his freedom. In such a situation the stalker gets stronger, not the victim.

In interpersonal cases, the stakes of intervention rise sharply. It is possible to identify cases in which intervention seemed to make the person go away and those in which intervention seemed to make the person escalate his pursuit. But if the question is one of safety, it is important to study attackers, the population who teaches us about those who act violently. Cases that escalate to violence have one factor in common alarmingly often: intervention.

It is common that TROs precede violence in stalking cases; this fact alone calls for the greatest caution when making that intervention decision. Study the cases, work back from the murder, and one will find police interventions or TROs, or both. There is plenty of support for caution:

- Laura Black—After four years of harassment and pursuit, Black finally served Richard Farley with a temporary restraining order, pending an official hearing one week later. On the morning of the hearing, Farley embarked on a bloody siege that lasted almost six hours, shooting ten people, including Black. Seven died in the attack. The restraining order that Black had initially opposed as provocative and that company officials advised her to seek ultimately propelled Farley from words to action.

- Ann Scripts—After years of alarming and violent incidents involving her husband, Scripps obtained a protection order. Her husband beat her to death two weeks later.
- Shirley Lowery—While waiting outside the courtroom for a TRO hearing, Lowery's husband stabbed her nineteen times.
- Kristen Lardner—Eleven days after getting a TRO, then an injunction, recommended by her sister, a lawyer, Lardner's ex-boyfriend killed her.
- Lynette Ruzillo—Four days after being served with a TRO, her husband attempted to kill her.
- Connie Chaney—She obtained a thirty-day protective order. Her husband raped her at gunpoint and attempted to kill her. So she got a two-year court order. Before gunning her down, he wrote in his diary, "THIS IS WAR."

This is a management strategy called "engage and enrage." But before that pattern unfolds, it is usually possible to try a less invasive management plan called "detach and watch." With this approach, the victim makes one explicit, unconditional rejection and then stops all contact.

In many cases, the attacker cited the TRO as the triggering factor. The reports of attackers or even the opinions of victims who survived attacks are not necessarily compelling evidence. Still, whether or not the TRO is accepted in a case of murder or attempted murder as a triggering factor, it clearly is not an effective or decisive factor in preventing the attack.

The whole idea behind stalker laws is to criminalize the conduct restraining orders seek to "restrain" so that victims do not need to seek civil action. The seeking of a TRO is essentially one party suing another. Like any lawsuit, a TRO has all the elements of a war. Conversely, stalking charges are the system, the society, the "People" against the stalker, not just a war between the stalker and the victim.

All states have laws that can be used to prosecute stalking behavior. Most states now have laws written specifically for stalking, but they vary widely in definition, requirements, and penalty. Some laws are more effective than others. In California, a stalker is defined as any person who willfully, maliciously, and repeatedly follows or harasses another person and who makes a credible threat with the intent to place that person in reasonable fear for his or her safety (Penal Code 646.9). Other states have similar laws.

Prosecution for many other crimes can also be effective management tools: arrests for trespassing (Penal Code 602 in California), prosecution for threats (Penal Code 422 in California), prosecution for telephone harassment (Penal Code 653-M in California), threat-trespass (Penal Code 603 in California), and several federal crimes under Title 18. No one law is appropriate for each case of stalking.

Criminal prosecution or a TRO is a management strategy that should be used only after all less invasive interventions have been tried, most notably detach and watch. With prosecution, it is important to have enough evidence to win the case. It is important to consider the likelihood of obtaining significant incarceration and/or other prohibitions, which will outweigh the possible escalation that this war might create. The victim should be prepared for the likelihood that the stalker will escalate his pursuit even after release from incarceration or the issuance of a TRO. The time immediately following issuance of the TRO is highly charged. Everything practical should be done to make the victim unavailable to the stalker.

If a person seeks a TRO because he/she believes the stalker is about to act violently, he/she has not done enough. As the judge in the Laura Black case noted after the attack, "This proves again that paper doesn't stop bullets." If it appears violence is imminent, important steps, other than court orders, are more urgently called for, most notably those that help make the victim unavailable to the stalker.

TROs and other confrontational interventions appeal to our sense of justice, and they appeal to victims, who feel they must do something to that person. It is important not to proceed with a management plan just because it appeals to the victim's sensibilities.

The desire to change the stalker is almost irresistible, but changing the victim's conduct is often more practical. Think of a slippery mountain road on a rainy night. You do not manage that hazard by getting out and drying off the pavement; you slow down through the dangerous curves. Law enforcement intervention is not appropriate for every case. Unfortunately, the overwhelming majority of cases of unwanted pursuit provide no opportunity for law enforcement intervention.

Police departments often recommend that victims seek TROs. Some outside law enforcement have misconstrued this to mean that TROs should be used in every case and that they stop harassment. Actually, they can be one part of an effective management plan. Ironically, it is precisely the fact that they do not stop some harassers that makes TROs valuable; they facilitate arrest and other interventions.

TROs and other confrontational interventions are often used in an effort to stop a stalker from sending letters. However, in some cases letters serve as an important emotional outlet for the stalker and thus should not be discouraged. The stop-the-letters goal is a common one. The existence and content of the letters often disturbs the victim and the people around the victim. To them it may seem that stopping the letters is stopping the problem.

However, letters are not in themselves dangerous, and though it is true that their impact can be emotionally harmful, that impact can also be controlled. This philosophy says that we change what we can change—those things under our control—and we recognize what we cannot change. There is no button that can be pushed to reliably improve the mental state of a stalker or control his conduct indefinitely. On the other hand, it is easy to stop reading the letters and to pass the task to someone else (such as professional threat assessors). The letters are important because they provide valuable information, such as the location of the stalker (through postmark) and continuing indications of his condition, circumstance, feelings, plans, action capability, and so forth.

When managing a stalking case, one is often strongly inclined to take some action, even if that action carries risks. In cases involving stalkers, however, restraint is sometimes necessary. Restraint is often thought of as inaction, but it is not: it is the application of a specific management plan. As with any important decision, the intervention options must be weighed against the likely benefits and costs.

Efforts to have a stalker hospitalized for mental health treatment or evaluation often have beneficial results, including the possibility that his condition will improve and his potentially dangerous ideation will subside. Other possible benefits might include the close supervision applied by the hospital, as well as notification of release. Finally, there is the peace the victim enjoys while the stalker is in the hospital. These gains might be persuasive, but it is also important to consider the possible costs, including giving his aggression a clearer focus, because he perceives that the victim put him in the hospital, and he is angry about it; validating his paranoid delusions, because now he has proof that people are out to get him; alienating him from developed sources of information, such as family members who may have assisted with the involuntary hospitalization; stigmatizing him as a dangerous person, which reduces his dignity and gives him even less to lose; and cementing obsessional ideation ("The more people who try to stop me, the more effort I must apply"). These possible risks are associated with seeking hospitalization and succeeding. Consider taking all of the same risks and failing. Since there are no guarantees, weighing that possibility is also important.

Interventions should be applied only when gains are likely or when no acceptable alternatives are available. It is important to avoid provoking action that might otherwise not have occurred.

It is possible in the earlier example that the stalker might write letters indefinitely and never do anything more intrusive. If so, then monitoring the letters for evidence that the situation might escalate is the response that best serves the safety goal in that particular situation. That strategy is not "doing nothing." Rather, it is making a reasoned decision to pursue a specific management plan.

Many management tools and preventive measures can be applied to enhance safety that are not detectable to the stalker. Some cases, however, might call for direct, even intrusive interventions, such as undertaking court action, seeking restraining orders and injunctions, arresting and taking custody of stalkers, transporting stalkers, petitioning mental hospitals and prisons for extended custody, misdirecting stalkers, and applying surveillance. Both engagement and detachment strategies have been successful, but neither approach is right for all cases.

Several cases of erotomania have been recorded, in which the obsessed person falsely believes a reciprocated love relationship exists. Some people assume that leading the stalker to believe that the object of his love is involved in another relationship might help. But this approach assumes too much: it assumes that mentally ill people will react just as healthy people would. It assumes that, like a jilted high school–age boyfriend, he will pout and then direct his interest elsewhere. It invests in the mentally ill stalker a degree of rationality that has not been demonstrated by his behavior.

Jim Hicklin was a popular radio personality in the early 1970s. Edward Taylor, an admiring listener, wrote him some letters that were overly chummy. The letters disturbed Hicklin to the point that he hired private investigators to deter Taylor from writing further. When this intervention dramatically worsened the situation, law enforcement interventions were applied. Taylor pursued a letter-writing campaign, making wild accusations against Hicklin. He said he felt threatened in his own home by the visits from detectives and police sent by Hicklin, so he purchased a gun for protection.

In April 1973, Hicklin embarked on a cruise vacation with his wife, which he announced on the air. Taylor, still having never met Hicklin, boarded the cruise ship and shot Hicklin to death in his wife's presence. Taylor is an excellent example of one who would not likely have become a murderer had he not become engaged into war. Doing something confrontational to the stalker seems right and appeals to our sense of justice, but if the fight is preventable, avoidance should be tried first, but never avoidance alone as a management plan.

Surveillance

Television shows and movies have (mis)taught that surveillance of the stalker is a reliable way to ensure the victim's safety. The reasoning is that if the stalker is observed en route to the victim, those following him can raise the alarm, thus allowing the victim to undertake some precaution quickly. Some people might even expect the surveillance team to intercept the stalker physically before he reaches his victim. In theory, this may be effective and practical; unfortunately, in practice, it is neither one. Given the life-safety stakes of managing stalking cases, it is important to apply surveillance only to those specific areas of case management in which it is likely to reliably serve the victim's well-being.

Surveillance is often misunderstood by people who believe it is a "solution" to inappropriate pursuit. It is not, because surveillances intended to monitor a person as a way to prevent attack pose a very high risk of worsening cases, since they are virtually invariably detected. The longer they go on, the greater that risk. Contrary to what is seen on television, a detective cannot sit outside someone's house undetected for days at a time and be certain the subject did not enter or exit through some alternate door or did not leave in some other car; in short, the detective really cannot be certain of anything. One-person surveillances do not work reliably. Professional surveillances run from upward of seven people. Surveillances directed toward organized crime figures, for example, take a large number of people in order that they not be detected. Private investigators, those usually called on to surveil stalkers, cannot be expected to have the resources, budget, or skill to conduct large-scale surveillances. Any small number of people on a surveillance will likely be detected or will lose the subject of the surveillance.

Stalkers who are mentally ill often have paranoid delusions or other delusions involving the victim. They may already believe that the victim or someone else is directly surveilling them, and to confirm it is to establish a kind of bond or connection with the victim that encourages hazard and discourages detachment (and detachment is, after all, the goal in managing any of these cases).

Even surveillances that remain undetected are subject to another serious problem: they cannot provide reliable indications of the location of the person who may pose a hazard. This is a problem because, knowing that surveillance is under way, victims have the misleading expectation that they are somehow "protected" and will reliably be notified in the event that the object of their concern moves toward them. Similarly, they expect to be reliably notified in the event that the subject is "lost" by the surveillance team, and such notification is rarely timely or reliable. These expectations provide a false and dangerous peace of mind.

The most common safety hazards that grow out of surveillances occur when the surveillance team loses the subject and chooses not to notify anyone until they have scurried around trying every alternative possible to determine whether they actually have lost the subject. It is during these panic sessions (as surveillance teams seek to find the person or just put off making the embarrassing phone call) that victims are at risk of unexpectedly encountering the very person who poses the hazard.

Surveillance is most valuable as an investigative tool or a supplement to adequate protective coverage, not as an alternative to security or a way to provide safety to clients. Surveillance is useful for learning about behavior; observing conduct and demeanor; confirming location or residence, vehicle type and description; determining or confirming employment; and so forth.

Information is valuable to an assessment, and surveillance can be an effective route to reliable information.

Periodic Monitoring

Inhibitors are a valuable assessment tool since most dangerous encounters are preceded by some detectable indicators. Individuals who act dangerously usually do so when they have little left to lose, and there are ways to observe the course of that process. It is important to develop "windows" to observe changes in an individual's situation and condition and periodically monitor the stalker to determine any changes to his/her level of inhibitors.

Monitoring and regular investigation should focus on possible changes in the stalker's situation and state of mind. This can be done through nonintrusive methods, including regular review and assessment of new communications or information. It is wise to be alert to any new information regarding a stalker's attitudes, mental state, situation, and location. Such information should be reviewed, maintained, and updated. New facts can be learned through continued monitoring and assessment of all material (letters, phone calls, etc.).

Toward this end, persons who might encounter the stalker or his communications should be advised to carefully document all information available and to retain all documents or items sent or delivered.

PREVENTION

Many options are available to help reduce the vulnerability to unwanted approaches and encounters. These strategies should be part of any management plan. They should also be utilized by anyone trying to decrease the likelihood of becoming a victim of stalking. Each of the following items are important because it is in combination that they provide an effective program.

Communicating clearly and explicitly is important, particularly when rejecting advances from another and when ending a relationship. When one person wants a relationship with another person who is not interested, the situation is not likely to be resolved to the satisfaction of both people. The likelihood of convincing the person who wants the relationship that it is a good idea not to pursue the relationship is as likely as a stalker convincing his victim that the relationship is a good idea.

Once the person who is ending the relationship has delivered one explicit rejection, there should be no further communication. An explicit rejection is a rejection that does not include any conditions. For example, if a woman were to tell someone she does not want to see him because she is not interested in having a relationship "right now," he may decide to wait until she is ready. To deliver an *explicit* rejection, she would say, for example, "I do not want a relationship with you."

Any further communication will be perceived as a negotiation. Negotiations are about possibilities. If it is not possible that the victim will change her mind, then there is nothing to talk about. Yet negotiate is exactly what people do for fear that he will get more upset if he gets no response or because people have learned in life that to achieve what you want, you must do something. In a stalking situation, almost any contact from the victim is perceived as progress. If the stalker calls thirty times, then the victim finally calls him back and tells him to stop, he just learned that the price of a return call is thirty calls. If the victim calls back eight times to tell him she wants nothing to do with him, she just entered into seven negotiations that betrayed her resolve, which is to stop contact. To stop contact, one must do exactly that: stop contact. There is no clearer way to communicate that no further contact with a person is desired than to stop communicating.

An early detection and notification system is an important part of prevention. Caution should be exercised when handling calls or letters from strangers. Strangers should never be provided with personal information or information about family, friends, and coworkers. Any information, no matter how minor it may appear, might encourage a person's pursuit or enable a successful encounter with the intended victim. Always take the name and telephone number of the person inquiring, stating that the message will be passed along to the appropriate person.

People at risk of stalking should ask others, including friends, family, coworkers, neighbors, and so on, that they wish to be notified if inquiries are made about them. Others should be part of efforts to learn about any individual who expresses an inappropriate interest. All such information should be documented and retained in the event it may be relevant to a future situation.

Taking measures to decrease accessibility to persons who might try to locate a residence address for the purpose of stalking is important. Part of this effort involves engaging the services of a private mailbox service. This "new" address becomes the official address on all records and in all address files.

Send postcards to friends, associates, family members, and others giving them the new address. Ask them to remove the old address from their files and Rolodexes and replace it with the new address. The new address is used on bank checks, registration records, and all other records.

Give a change-of-address card to all current creditors who would have the actual home address. Provide them with the mailbox address. Some credit reporting agencies will remove past addresses from credit histories if requested; such a request should be made.

Often, private investigators or others utilize credit history information to locate people. To help detect this, enroll in TRW Credential Service so that the consumer is notified whenever any credit inquiry is conducted regarding them.

Credit account information is also used for marketing purposes. Credit bureaus frequently release information from individual credit files to companies that offer "preapproved" credit cards or other lines of credit. California law mandates that any company that accesses credit account information must disclose that practice to the consumer; the company must also advise of the right to prohibit further such use of credit report information. Request that credit bureaus remove the name from these lists.

Real property should be placed in a trust rather than the victim's name. This also applies to cable companies and other services such as newspaper delivery. Information gathered by utility providers can be utilized by individuals seeking to locate others.

Utility providers, telephone companies, and other household service companies will usually assign a code word to an account, if requested. This precaution would require that anyone calling for information about an individual's account, or attempting to make changes to the account, have the code word.

Telephone numbers should be unlisted or unpublished. Further, since telephones are a critical area of reducing vulnerability to stalking, it is sometimes beneficial to have present home telephone numbers disconnected and service restarted under a new name at that address. (It is not a good idea to disconnect the telephone lines of a current stalking victim. Rather, transfer the current number to a voice mail account and establish a new number for appropriate calls. This enables continued monitoring for information about the stalker, who eventually is the only person calling that number.)

Take precautions to avoid the home address being given out for work-related reasons. The private mailbox address should be sufficient for an employer. Urgent information can be sent via facsimile or delivered to the mailbox address. If something must be messengered to the home, establish a fictitious name that can be used, or the homeowner should have the material picked up by a service, so that the residence address does not appear on the receipt left with the sender.

Avoid being followed from predictable places such as work locations or the private mailbox. This measure can be as simple as increasing awareness of nearby people and surrounding vehicles.

Carefully review all public and private records, such as fictitious business filings/court records, banking records, pet licensing records, and voter registration. For example, registered voters should be aware that their name and address could be made available to persons trying to locate them.

Security measures, such as a security alarm and early warning systems, should be installed at residences. The importance of dogs cannot be overstated. Additional security improvements can include such things as how a person walks from the car to the house (preferably within a closed garage) and use of an access control system (intercom, camera, etc.). Simple precautions such as not being alone while walking to the car at predictable places go a long way toward reducing the likelihood of an unmanageable encounter.

Self-defense classes such as IMPACT Personal Safety and Model Mugging offer several advantages. These programs are beneficial in teaching self-defense techniques and improving self-confidence, which is reflected in how a person carries him- or herself.

A public figure should review the overall process for handling fan mail. Generally speaking, it is a bad idea to respond automatically to all fan mail. If the public figure chooses to respond to fan mail from the general public, then it should be according to established criteria, such as teenagers who were inspired by their work or children with disabilities. These responses can be personal and specific responses. Without this criteria, the public figure has no control over who receives the response or the reaction to it.

In this day and age, media figures should not respond to those people who are looking for personal contact. To illustrate the importance of this recommendation regarding fan mail, we need only look to the very public case of Robert Bardo, who killed actress Rebecca Schaeffer. Bardo himself has said that the letter he received from Schaeffer was very encouraging to his pursuit. He now advocates that public figures do not respond to their mail: "If you do answer fan mail, don't let it be so overglowing. That's not the way to be with a fan, because it makes it seem like they're the only one, and that's how I felt. I felt I was the only one." (de Becker, 1997, p. 242).

This is not to say that fan mail should be discarded; it should not. These communications are very important for discovering, assessing, and monitoring those people who might inappropriately pursue public figures. Inappropriate material should be assessed, investigated, and documented. Appropriate material can simply be thrown away after the names and addresses are recorded.

These preventive efforts increase safety and privacy and help prevent the likelihood of becoming a victim of stalking. They also help current victims become less accessible to stalkers.

Protective Services: Critical Issues for Selection

Resources are generally more wisely allocated to protective coverage as opposed to surveillance. A protective detail, or an increase in an already established protective detail, should often be used in lieu of a two-person surveillance team. This approach serves as a "net" that has a higher likelihood of catching both the individual who poses concern as well as any other individuals who might pursue unwanted encounters.

The most critical issue regarding protective coverage is choosing a reliable, competent, and qualified service. For starters, the security firm should perform thorough screening and background investigations of all employees. The screening should include tests, multiple interviews, urinalysis for detection of drug use, a polygraph test to confirm the accuracy of information provided during the employment process, and a complete background investigation, including interviews of every former employer and reference.

The security firm also should maintain a staff of full-time professionals whose training and careers are dedicated to protective coverage. Part-time personnel are often dedicated to their primary jobs, they have often already worked eight or ten hours by the time they reach their security assignment, and they are often not as dedicated to the most recent training and licensing. The use of part-time personnel does not encourage uniformity of service or professionalism.

The security firm should maintain a sophisticated and ongoing training program. Its training program should be directed by a professional with experience in training. Personnel should be well versed in first aid, arrest techniques and retention, firearms use, safety, self-defense, security systems, and communications equipment. They should be familiar with stalking issues and up-to-date on the relevant laws and public policies.

The security firm should be able to immediately produce the actual test scores and documentation of training for each and every person they employ. If a firm cannot share its training program, such a program probably does not exist.

The security firm should be licensed by the state department that regulates security services. Its record should be available for review and free of disciplinary actions or revocations. Most states require that every guard maintain a registration with the state. This is issued after the employee successfully completes a state test and passes a criminal records check. Confirm that each employee has a valid state registration card, and determine whether the state has ever rejected the applications of employees or candidates submitted by the firm.

The security firm should carry at least double the state-required liability insurance. It should have policies covering worker's compensation for all employees, full medical coverage for all employees, as well as special policies covering the vehicles used to transport clients. If the firm has never had a claim against its liability policy, its insurer should be glad to name a client as a coinsured party.

The security firm should have strict physical condition requirements. Working protective coverage requires that personnel be in peak physical condition, with strength, agility, and speed appropriate to the challenges that might arise. Be sure policy requiring fitness is accompanied by a testing program that ensures compliance. The results of those regular tests should be available for review.

The security firm should demand that employees sign confidentiality agreements. A dedication to the privacy of clients is a clear requirement. It should be enforced by a contract that prohibits employees and former employees from disclosing any information about clients.

The security firm should have written policies covering firearms use, arrests, and other critical aspects of protective coverage. All employees should understand and strictly apply them.

The security firm should continue to evaluate its personnel on an ongoing basis. Service firms in any field rely on the dedication and ability of their personnel. In this sensitive area, employees should have regular evaluations of their performance and fitness for the job. These measures should include random urinalysis to guarantee drug-free personnel; close supervisory scrutiny, documented by written evaluations; carefully maintained and reviewed personnel files; and salary package incentives that are tied to performance and ability, not seniority. Frequent bonuses and rewards should be tempered by a clearly understood disciplinary policy.

The security firm should specialize in protective coverage. If the firm's "bread and butter" is providing security guards for warehouses, guards at grocery stores, or uniformed patrol staff, then it does not likely have the best experience or resource for executive protection.

Finally, select a security firm whose history and reputation is built on delivering this specialized type of protective coverage and logistical support. Pick a firm whose training, equipment, management, and day-to-day operations focus on this specialized area.

There is no one easy answer to stalking cases. Serious stalking cases should be professionally assessed and managed. Even the most serious cases are predictable, preventable, and manageable.

6

CRISIS AND HOSTAGE NEGOTIATIONS

Community and Corporate Responses to Violent Incidents

FREDERICK J. LANCELEY

There is no one place for a crisis of violence, as we have all seen in the newspapers and on TV. A violent incident can happen in the home, a school, the workplace, a public institution, a private business—just about anywhere. It happens suddenly, generally without warning, and the worst possible response is panic, as understandable as such a reaction might be. This chapter deals with strategies for responding to a violent crisis in a manner that will prevent its escalation, which might well result in tragedy.

FIRST-RESPONDER NEGOTIATIONS

It is 8:30 A.M. You have arrived at your office. Your secretary is already in, but with her is her ex-husband. He has a knife to her throat and shouts at you, "If I can't have her, nobody will!"

How would you respond? How would your employees respond? The first hour of any violent crisis is the most volatile, and law enforcement agencies typically take about an hour to set up their crisis management team. Therefore, the responsibility for managing this dangerous, pivotal hour, which often governs the course of the entire incident, often falls on non–law enforcement personnel.

First-responder negotiations may be likened to first aid. They are crucial when something has to be done until the trained professionals arrive. None of us would allow the victim of an accident or crime to slowly bleed to death because we are not doctors or emergency medical technicians. We would try to do something. Likewise, first-responder negotiations represent an attempt to prevent a violent incident from developing into something even worse. First-responder negotiations, then, are *not* intended to replace negotiations by a trained negotiator; they should be used primarily as an effective holding strategy until help from trained law enforcement negotiators and tactical teams arrives.

The ultimate goal of the first responder is to prevent or reduce the likelihood of further violence. The initial actions of the responder should be directed toward calming the perpetrator and stablizing the situation—that is, preventing the threat from spreading. First responders should bear in mind that almost invariably anxiety and fear are the predominant emotions being experienced by the perpetrator. Anger is also very common; so, above everything else, the first responder must ensure his or her own safety. This consideration cannot be emphasized too strongly.

Do's and Don'ts in First-Responder Negotiations

Whenever possible, the first responder should begin to clear the area of employees and others, removing them to a place of safety. The evacuated persons should be taken to a holding area for debriefing by law enforcement personnel, a procedure that may prove vitally important for later negotiations and tactical efforts, as well as eventual prosecution. Another concern, in certain situations, involves any people who may be trapped by the perpetrator's actions but whose presence he is not aware of. This is a very tricky situation, and the authorities should be informed of it as soon as they arrive. Meanwhile, first responders should not reveal to the perpetrator that they know anything about it. (The masculine pronoun is used throughout this chapter to identify the perpetrator of a violent incident, as by far the greatest majority of such incidents are instigated by men. Keep in mind, however, that women, too, are perpetrators, and, in any case, these general tips on how to act in such situations are not gender-specific.)

Generally, such as in the vignette opening this chapter, the first responder has no choice but to make the initial contact with the offender. During this initial contact, the first responder should concentrate on trying to calm the offender, develop additional information, buy time, and in one way or another keep him busy.

In some cases, it is the first responder who decides on his or her own to initiate contact with the perpetrator. In this instance, the first responder should concentrate on reassuring the offender that things are under control and that no one is going to try to come in after him. In any case, first responders should avoid soliciting any demands. Basically, the initial statements by first responders may set the tone for the next few hours. A first responder might begin by saying:

> Hello in there. My name is _____ with _____ . Everything is under control out here. Is everything all right in there?

In all cases, it is more important to be a good listener than a good talker. Listening carefully to the offender's responses may provide the first responder with valuable information about the situation because everything the offender says will tell the intervener something about him. For instance, just listening to the offender may give the first responder an idea of what is important to him and what it will take to get him out of there. At this stage, bargaining with or making concessions to the offender should be avoided, so while listening, the first responder should try to avoid offering anything.

More important, letting the offender talk not only provides information but may help reduce his anxiety, one of the key goals of the initial contact. Moreover, while the offender is talking, the first responder is gaining time. (The mere passage of time may be the most important goal to achieve during this stage; the importance of the passage of time will be discussed in detail later in this chapter.)

When talking to the offender, the first responder shouldn't try too quickly to "push the deal" (i.e., make a resolution or compromise). Few of us trust someone who is pushing a deal on us before we are ready. This feeling is especially true of those who, like the perpetrator, are fearful and tense to begin with. First responders should also avoid giving orders or making demands that may escalate the confrontation.

It is important for the first responder to take notes on events and conversations as they occur and to note the time of each occurrence. This can also prove invaluable later on. Many negotiators in a crisis situation feel that they will be able to reconstruct events at a later time and fail to keep a log. They are shocked to realize when the time comes that they cannot remember what was said or done, why actions were taken or not taken, or what the sequence of events actually was.

Also, first responders generally attempt to minimize the seriousness of the attempted crime when speaking to law officers or other outsiders. They may say, for example, "Nothing much has happened. No one has been hurt [or killed]." Or, when asked about a victim's condition, they may say, "I don't know his condition because I've been talking with you."

Most important, trust is critical to the establishment of a rapport with the perpetrator, and nothing will destroy the rapport-building process faster than being caught in a lie or trick. As a result, first responders must strive to be as honest as possible and to avoid tricks.

First responders and negotiators should also avoid directing frequent attention to the victims. They should not even call them hostages. Calling the victims "hostages" may lead the offender to believe he has bargaining power, and directing frequent attention to the victims may also lead the offender to believe he has more power than he really does. Instead, first responders should attempt to get him involved with themselves rather than increasing his involvement with the victims. However, it may be appropriate, in the early stages, to ask for the names and condition of all those under the offender's control. Here negotiators and first responders may try to personalize the hostages or victims by using their names if known.

During this initial stage, if first responders are not sure what an offender means by some statement or demand, they should ask him for clarification, always being sure to use good judgment. They should *not* ask an offender to clarify a vague threat, and they should never dismiss any request (or demand) as trivial. If the perpetrator brings it up, it is important to him. Discussing seemingly small issues will keep him talking, allow time to pass, and set a precedent for working together. At the same time, first responders should never say no to a demand. Remember, not saying no does not mean saying yes. The attitude is "We will discuss anything." In response to requests or demands, tell the offender, "I understand and will pass it on" or "Someone is working on that right now."

First responders are not decision makers, and they should not present themselves as the final authority in an incident. On the other hand, they must avoid using terms such as "my boss," "my supervisor," or "the director of the company." If such terms are used, the common response of the perpetrator is to ask for the person named. First responders certainly do not want to present themselves as any kind of final authority, but they do not want to set up another individual as the final authority, either. First responders should say things such as, "I'll check with ['the home office,' 'corporate headquarters,' 'New York,' or some other impersonal entity or group of decision makers]."

If demands are being made, the first responder should attempt to soften the demands. For example, the offender might say, "I want my job back and a $10,000 raise." A first responder or negotiator should say, "Okay, I understand you are concerned about your job. I'll pass that along and make sure someone starts looking into it as soon as the others get here." If the offender is making demands, first responders should not make alternative suggestions to him, and they should never, in response to any demand, allow for any exchange of hostages.

First responders should never set a deadline on themselves or tell the offender that something will be done within a specific time frame. For example, a first responder should not say, "I'll have some coffee for you in ten minutes." Deadlines, even self-imposed deadlines, are often difficult to meet despite the best of intentions. When the deadlines are not met, offenders tend to think it is because the negotiator or first responder is trying to trick him.

First responders should not introduce "outsiders"—namely, the offender's friends, family, lawyer, doctor, clergy, and others. Using third-party intermediaries is a tricky business and has probably precipitated more violence than any other single negotiating tactic. For example, unbeknownst to law enforcement at the time, fathers have been put on the telephone with daughters they had previously raped. Family members and girlfriends have encouraged suicides. Wives' lovers have been put on the telephone to talk to outraged, homicidal husbands. When such outsiders are put on the telephone, it is hard to predict what they will say despite what they tell the first responder beforehand. Friends, relatives, and others almost always arrive on the scene and insist that they can talk the offender out. The tricky part about using third-party intermediaries is in determining when it will work and when it will lead to tragedy. This decision is best left to experienced negotiators.

If a first responder senses he or she is in a possible suicide situation, he should ask the offender about it directly: "Are you thinking of committing suicide?" Every major suicide or crisis hot line in the United States considers this question essential to suicide intervention. Though first responders often find it difficult to bring the subject up, they should not feel they will push the offender over the edge or put the idea into his head. Often, suicide is an issue both parties know exists, and approaching the topic directly and openly is the best course. It will then be out in the open and available for discussion. It is very likely that the offender has broached the subject of suicide with friends and relatives, and they have either refused to discuss it with him or else made light of it. The negotiator's willingness to discuss suicide will go a long way toward establishing rapport.

In this regard, first responders should be aware of a phenomenon known as "suicide by cop," a situation in which an offender wants to die but does not want to do it himself. Instead, he wants the police or someone else to kill him. Virtually all suicidal people can be dangerous, but those contemplating suicide by cop can be especially so because they will kill innocent victims to provoke the police or others into killing them. A bank teller was killed on designated deadline when the police did not comply with the offender's demand to be killed within thirty minutes. After killing the teller, the offender stepped in front of a window knowing full well that a police sniper was across the street. He was killed by the sniper.

All crisis situations involve peril, and first responders should *never* expose themselves to possible danger to negotiate face-to-face, especially if the offender has a firearm. When speaking to an armed offender, the interveners must be sure that they are in a position of cover and that they understand the difference between cover and concealment. "Cover" will stop a bullet. "Concealment" is something to hide behind. A brick wall may provide adequate cover. An azalea bush may provide concealment but not cover.

First responders must also be ready for success. The early surrender of an offender is always a possibility, and they should plan for it early on. First responders do not want to get into a situation in which they have to tell the offender to stay where he is because the people outside are not ready to receive him. If first responders are doing so well, in that they have developed a rapport with the offender, many law enforcement agencies will allow them to continue after the police have arrived. The law enforcement agency will sit by the side of the first responder and coach him or her through the ordeal.

Lastly, when making decisions, remember the words of Lieutenant Robert Louden, New York City Police Department (retired): "Safety and control must always be the prime considerations in the decision-making process." No decisions should be made that will increase risk to *anyone* or loosen the community's control of the situation.

Preparing for First-Responder Situations

The Federal Bureau of Investigation (FBI) and other law enforcement agencies have been teaching what they call "first-responder negotiations" to law enforcement agencies for about ten years. The idea behind this approach is simply that if responding patrol officers can effectively handle the incident at the outset, the situation may not evolve into something not only more dangerous but more expensive in terms of manpower and overtime costs. In fact, law enforcement agencies have successfully employed first-response negotiations in a variety of circumstances such as those involving hostage taking, barricaded perpetrators, and domestic violence.

I have been training corporate security and human resources personnel for some time to respond effectively to violent incidents in the workplace and have seen firsthand the significant benefits such preparations can bring to the community and corporations. An effective response during the first few minutes to an hour calms the perpetrator faster, thereby reducing the likelihood of violence or further violence; enhances the probability of a peaceful outcome; decreases workplace downtime; makes the transition to law enforcement agencies easier; and lessens trauma on employees.

Unfortunately, communities, corporations, and even law enforcement agencies find it difficult to spend money on training for unlikely events. None of us wants to believe that a mechanism for managing violent incidents is necessary in our workplace. Yet, violence is a daily occurrence in our society. I recently gave a presentation on managing violence in Charleston, South Carolina, during which an interested acquaintance said that there was never any violence in his workplace except, of course, for the occasional fistfight. Violence is so common in our society we have become inured to it.

NEGOTIATING A CRISIS SITUATION: THE INTENT

Violence comes in many forms, and in managing an incident it is crucial to determine the offender's motivation. A confounding factor in determining motivation is the lack of precision in our vocabulary. For example, not all those held against their will are hostages, but we often hear in the media that someone is being held hostage. Using the term *hostage* strictly as done in this chapter, however, we find that true hostage situations are relatively rare. This section sets forth some more precise terminology and so gives crisis negotiators a better perspective on what is actually happening in an incident.

Consider the following scenarios: an ex-husband is holding his former wife at gunpoint because she insisted on a divorce; an embassy is taken over by terrorists who are pressuring for the release of their comrades from prison; an armed robber in a convenience store is telling police that unless they shoot him, he is going to shoot his captive; a subject enters a residence in the middle of the night and abducts a baby for which the parents later receive a ransom demand; and a teenage gunman walks into a classroom, captures twenty of his classmates, and demands pizzas and Cokes. Upon arrest all of these individuals will, most probably, be prosecuted for the violation of a state or federal kidnapping statute, and, as such, all may be considered kidnappers. Under the federal kidnapping statute, Title 18, United States Code, Section 1201, "whoever unlawfully seizes, confines, inveigles, decoys, kidnaps, abducts, or carries away and holds for ransom or reward or otherwise any person . . . shall be punished by imprisonment for any term of years or for life." The statute tells us who may be prosecuted under the statute but tells us very little about the offender's motivation. Some states have statutes specifically for situations in which victims are being held against their will. These statutes are generally called "unlawful detention," "false imprisonment," or something similar.

Negotiating a Kidnapping: For Ransom, Reward, or Otherwise

The *American Heritage Dictionary of the English Language* defines the transitive verb *kidnap* as "to abduct and detain (a person or animal), often for ransom." Notice that this definition says "often for ransom." Both the statute mentioned earlier and the definition of kidnapping acknowledge that kidnappings do not always involve ransoms. Thus, an incident does not have to include a demand for ransom to qualify as a kidnapping.

The kidnapper who "holds for reward or ransom" perpetrates a crime that is relatively straightforward in terms of motivation. The kidnapper is generally motivated by the desire for monetary gain, and the intent is to achieve that goal. The "otherwise" kidnappers are the ones who cause law enforcement the most difficulty in terms of understanding their motivation and thereby procuring a handle for managing and controlling the incident.

To understand an offender's motivation, crisis negotiators must ask themselves throughout the incident, "What is the offender's intent?" Negotiators must continue asking this question throughout the incident because (1) the answer is not always apparent and (2) the offender's intent may change. In fact, crisis negotiators want the offender's intent to change.

There are two variations of the crime prosecuted as a kidnapping: those in which a victim is held in a location known to the authorities, and those in which a victim is held in a location unknown to the authorities. Either form of kidnapping may or may not result in a substantive demand. *If there is a substantive demand in return for the promised release of the abducted individual, that particular kind of victim is a hostage.* (A substantive demand is one that the hostage taker could not have achieved by himself.) If there is no substantive demand made upon the authorities or other party, the person held is a captive or victim but not a hostage.

Kidnapping: Unknown Location

In a Latin American country, a young man was abducted, taken to a still unknown location, and his father received a demand for $20 million. In this situation, the kidnapper's motivation is obvious; he wants the money. In a kidnapping in which the victim is taken to an unknown location and there is a substantive demand, the kidnapped person is a particular kind of victim called a hostage (see Figure 6.1). A *hostage* is defined as a person held and threatened by an offender to force the fulfillment of substantive demands by a third party. Notice that this definition of hostage makes no mention of the location of the victim but does mention substantive demands. Typical substantive demands are for ransom (usually money) or some political, social, or religious change. True hostage situations require bargaining by their very nature. Without a substantive demand, there is no hostage situation but law enforcement may be facing an equally or more dangerous situation.

In South Carolina, a woman was abducted from her front yard. Sometime later her body was found in a wooded area. She

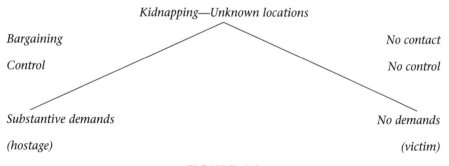

Kidnapping—Unknown locations

| *Bargaining* | *No contact* |
| *Control* | *No control* |

Substantive demands   *No demands*

(hostage)   *(victim)*

FIGURE 6.1

had been sexually assaulted, tortured, and murdered. Her assailant could have been charged with kidnapping as well as other offenses.

If the kidnap victim is taken to an unknown location and no ransom demand is made, that victim is not a hostage by definition. If there is no ransom demand, why was the kidnapping carried out? These are the "otherwise" kidnappings. Kidnappers do not perpetrate their crimes unless the act benefits them in some way. Any number of motives or purposes are possible: sexual assault, abuse, or exploitation; child stealing; romance; a custodial or domestic dispute; religious or cult considerations; deprogramming; political considerations; narcotic involvements; retribution; transportation in connection with another crime; or a host of other reasons.

Kidnapping: Known Location

In the movie *Dog Day Afternoon*, victims are being held in a bank. The bank robbers want to trade the victims for transportation out of the country. These victims are hostages. Before the aircraft hijacking statute was passed, aircraft hijackers were charged with violation of the federal kidnapping law. Now aircraft hijackers are kidnappers, and their victims are hostages.

Kidnappings in locations known to the authorities may or may not result in substantive demands. *A subset of kidnappers who make substantive demands and are holding their victims in known locations are called hostage takers* (see Figure 6.2). Substantive demands being made from a known location are identical to those being made from an unknown location except that now there is often an escape demand. An escape demand is necessary because the authorities know where the *kidnapper* is located. For example, an armed robber is trapped in a convenience store by a rapid police response, and he wants a getaway car. Terrorists aboard a hijacked aircraft are demanding freedom for their imprisoned comrades and themselves. The armed robber could not escape by himself, and the terrorists could not effect the release of their associates without assistance from the authorities. These events are

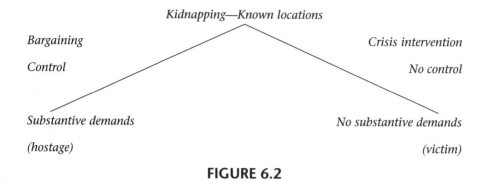

FIGURE 6.2

hostage situations. Negotiators in such situations usually have a rather clear idea of the perpetrators' motives.

On the other hand, consider an offender holding several people at gunpoint and demanding soft drinks, pizza, and cigarettes. Could he have achieved his demands without holding people and without the assistance of the authorities? Obviously, there are easier ways to get pizza, drinks, and cigarettes. Other nonsubstantive, and quite common, demands include demands for alcohol, coffee, or the like. These demands are within the reach of anyone, so why is the offender holding his captives? Something else is going on in the offender's mind besides a desire for fast food and cigarettes. This is not, by definition, a hostage situation, and it is vital for negotiators and law enforcement people to determine what is driving the incident.

In April 1979, in a lecture to his students, Harvey Schlossberg, Ph.D. (New York City Police Department, retired), observed that a hostage taker is not there to kill his victims. He is there to get his demands met. Dr. Schlossberg's words are as true today as they were then. Hostage takers are not there to kill their victims, but a would-be-murderer may *look* like a hostage taker, and unless negotiators are able to determine his real intention, their negotiations will miss the point and be ineffective. Negotiators must continually ask themselves, "Is there an easier way to get this demand met?" In the case of relatively trivial demands, they must be sensitive to a possible other agenda, maybe a homicidal impulse or homicidal/suicidal intent. They must be aware of the situation; for example, victims are sometimes hiding and the offender is not sure where they are. On other occasions, it may be that the innocent persons are present because they want to be and there is no real threat to them.

On the other hand, in the scene at the beginning of this chapter in which the man was holding his wife at knifepoint, there were no substantive demands, so what did the offender want? The answer is nothing. The offender has what he wants! The offender may have one or more intentions, uses, or purposes for the captive such as sexual assault, abuse, or exploitation, humiliation, homicide/suicide, or gain a captive audience for his suicide. At such times, the interveners must determine what is behind the offender's actions.

Putting Figures 6.1 and 6.2 together to form Figure 6.3 illustrates a number of interesting points. Hostage situations, on the

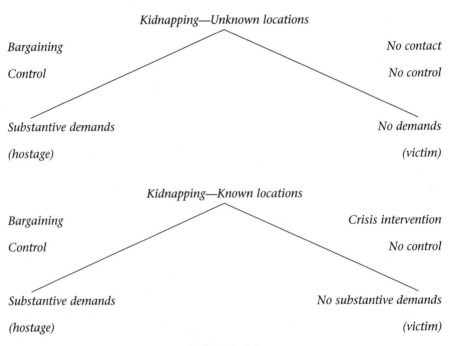

FIGURE 6.3

left side of Figure 6.3, involve bargaining because the victim was taken for his or her value in trade. Trading and bargaining in true hostage situations are, therefore, to be expected. On the other hand, because the offender wants something, negotiators are not powerless. They have some control.

On the right side of Figure 6.3 are the nonhostage situations. These incidents are not motivated by a need to get something from the authorities, so no bargaining is done. If the location of the victim is known, these incidents tend to be more emotional, and as a result crisis intervention techniques come more into play. On the upper-right side of Figure 6.3, we have nonhostage situations in which people have been abducted and are being held against their will. If the victim has been taken to an unknown location and the authorities have no contact with the offender, there is not much the authorities can do but look for them.

On the lower-right side of Figure 6.3, we also have non-hostage situations. In these known-location situations, the offender may not want to talk to the authorities but he generally does, eventually. In this situation, he does not want anything from the authorities, so there is no bargaining. Crisis intervention techniques are employed in this kind of situation rather than hostage negotiation techniques. In essence, the negotiator becomes a crisis intervener. Hostage negotiation is crisis intervention with bargaining techniques added. If we take the bargaining out of a hostage negotiation, we are left with crisis intervention.

Today's crisis negotiators must respond to a wide variety of incidents, including kidnapping. It is important for negotiators to understand that there is more than one form of prosecutable kidnapping—those at known locations and those at unknown locations—and either form may result in a demand. It is critical to know that some kidnapped persons are hostages and others are potential murder victims. It is also vital to fully understand these differentiations because the circumstances of the crime so directly reflect the offender's intent and the possible outcome of an incident. The offender's purpose for holding an abducted individual will have a direct bearing on how a negotiation is conducted, the necessity for tactical action, and how the incident is managed.

HOSTAGE NEGOTIATIONS

Hostage negotiation, as a discipline, began in the New York City Police Department in the early 1970s. Shortly after New York City began its program, the FBI began one of its own. Thanks to Harvey Schlossberg, Ph.D. and Captain Frank Bolz, both now retired from the New York City Police Department, and the FBI, every major police department in the United States has developed a hostage negotiation team.

Since the 1970s, hostage negotiators have experienced a remarkable record of success. Surprisingly, no nationwide statistics on hostage situations or their outcomes are available, but experienced hostage negotiators in seminars at the FBI Academy have consistently estimated a very high success rate. If the nonviolent resolution of hostage situations is so common in such major cities as New York, Houston, Los Angeles, and Chicago, we should ask, "Why are we so successful?" From that question arises another: "Are there identifiable elements in a hostage situation that might indicate when the odds of success are less than favorable?" Before attempting to assess whether a hostage situation is negotiable, we should determine whether the incident is actually a hostage situation. This determination is achieved by defining our terms.

To *negotiate* is to arrange or settle by conferring or discussing, which is precisely what negotiators attempt to do in a hostage situation. Hostage negotiators are not mediators. Mediators are generally viewed as neutral. Hostage negotiators are not neutral because they are paid by and are representing the city, county, state, or federal government. Negotiators trying to appear neutral will lose credibility with the hostage taker because he knows the negotiator is a cop even though he is not acting like one. Acting neutral may even cost credibility with or the confidence of others on the crisis management team because they may fear that the negotiator's objectivity has been lost. Negotiators can only maintain the confidence of both sides by being both firm and empathetic—but within their role of law enforcement officers.

Negotiators at the FBI Academy are taught the "Eight Elements of Hostage Negotiation," described in the following subsections, and use them in their assessment of an incident.

1. A Need to Live on the Part of the Hostage Taker

Hostage negotiation techniques presuppose that the hostage taker has a need to live; that is, they presuppose that the hostage taker wants something that he cannot achieve by himself, a substantive demand, and that he wants to live to enjoy the fruits of his crime.

Negotiators often express concern about provoking the hostage taker lest he kill the hostage. Yet the hostage taker, if he has a need to live, cannot provoke the authorities too much, either. The hostage taker hopes to provoke the authorities just enough to get his demands met, but not so much that they feel compelled to use overwhelming deadly force against him. (Previously discussed were the situations in which the intent is suicide by cop, not gain. This is a very dangerous situation and requires crisis negotiation techniques that differ from hostage negotiation. Thus, determining early the offender's intent is vital to managing the situation. In the following discussion, we will largely assume that the intent is to live and profit from the abduction.)

If a hostage taker has a need to live but recognizes that his demands will not be met, he does not have many remaining options. One option is to kill a hostage out of spite, frustration, or as a last-ditch effort to get demands met. He knows, however, that if he employs this option, the authorities are likely to use deadly force against him. If he has a need to live, killing a hostage becomes an option he rationally cannot risk. Having failed in getting the authorities to meet his demands and fearing the use of deadly force by the authorities, surrender becomes the hostage taker's remaining alternative.

2. A Threat of Force by the Authorities

The offender must appreciate the fact that the authorities have a force option available to them. The threat of force must be a viable one; that is, the offender must perceive that the force option is available to the authorities, that he is vulnerable to it, and that the authorities are willing to employ it should they deem it necessary. If even one of these perceptions is missing, the threat of force will be a hollow one.

In general, it is better to play down a threat of force in order to reduce the offender's anxiety, but he must know it is there. The hostage taker does not want to provoke the force option because he has a need to live, and the force option would jeopardize his life. When the authorities employ the force option, the incident is over, and the hostage taker knows that, whatever else happens, his demands will not be met. He knows that the authorities always prevail in siege situations that end in a shootout. The authorities may suffer losses, even severe losses, but the end result is almost invariably the arrest, or even death, of the offender.

The threat of force element is equally valid in international hostage situations. The offending government or terrorist group must realize that the victim government has a force option available, the offenders are vulnerable, and the victim government has the will to employ the force option. If the hostage taker feels no threat, he has nothing to lose and everything to gain by holding hostages.

For example, during the Carter administration Americans were taken hostage in Teheran, Iran. The Iranian government knew that the United States government had a force option available. They knew, too, that if a missile were launched at them, there was nothing they could do to protect themselves from the action. What they did not believe was that President Carter would take such overwhelming tactical action.

Enter Ronald Reagan and his message: nuclear wars are winnable. There is talk of using nuclear weapons tactically. Reagan becomes president, and on the day he is inaugurated the hostages are released. Why? Because President Reagan *might* take the actions the Iranian government did not fear under President Carter.

3. Communication between the Hostage Taker and the Authorities

In a hostage situation, the hostage taker must communicate his demands and threats to someone. The "someone" is generally the authorities but could be any party capable of fulfilling the hostage taker's demands—for example, newspapers or television and radio stations that were told to broadcast a manifesto or air a grievance in return for a hostage's life. Television and radio stations have been taken over in Phoenix and Cleveland as well as elsewhere. One might even say that the so-called "Unabomber," who threatened to continue killing unless his manifesto was published in a leading newspaper, was holding the American public hostage. Without the communication of demands to a third party, the incident is a private dispute. There is no such thing as a secret hostage taking. A demand and threat must be communicated.

The person or entity who is confronted by the hostage taker must care about the lives of the hostages. If the extorted party expresses and feels no concern about the threat to the hostages, the hostage taker has nothing with which to bargain. It is only the *caring* about the hostage that gives the hostage taker his power. For example, many of us can remember that troubled time when Americans were being held hostage in Teheran, but how many of us can remember what Iran's leader at the time said when Iranians were taken hostage in Iran's London Embassy? Essentially, he said the hostages should be proud to die for the revolution. Where does that leave the hostage takers? The Iranians were rescued due to the caring of the London Metropolitan Police and the British military.

4. A Leader or Decision-Making Process among the Hostage Takers

The failure of one of the hostage takers to assume a leadership role or the failure of a decision-making process to develop among the hostage takers can make a negotiated resolution an extremely difficult, if not impossible, goal to attain. If a single leader emerges among the hostage takers, the authorities seek to influence him, so that he makes the decisions they want. He should be someone who not only can make decisions but who can enforce his decisions among the other hostage takers. He should also be someone the authorities can hold personally accountable for his actions and the actions of the other hostage takers.

At the Atlanta penitentiary siege in November and early December 1987, negotiators were having a difficult time determining who was in charge among the Cuban detainees. Actually, two problems were present. First, the detainees were split among several factions so there was no one leader among them. Second, many of the detainees had experienced prison time in the Cuban system. It took a while for negotiators to understand that in Cuba when a disturbance occurred in a prison, the authorities would expend a great deal of effort in determining who was responsible for the disturbance. After such a determination was made, the inmate leadership was punished severely. So, when FBI negotiators in Atlanta asked who was in charge, several detainees insisted that they were not leaders.

If no one person emerges in a leadership position, the authorities should look for a decision-making process so that the process as opposed to an individual can be influenced. Individual and/or group decision making will take place among the hostage takers, and the more the authorities can influence the decision-making process, the higher the likelihood of a successful resolution. In the past, the authorities have successfully used the tactic of dropping leaflets or speaking to large groups over loudspeakers to ensure that all of the hostage takers or their followers hear the government's position. Again, at the Atlanta penitentiary, authorities, sensing that not all of the detainees were receiving the government's message, decided to reach out to all of the detainees. The crisis management team set up loudspeakers and printed leaflets telling all of the detainees the government's position.

Sometimes coherent negotiations are impossible. In a small Midwestern county jail, an overweight deputy sheriff with a heart problem was taken hostage by several inmates. Each of the inmates had his own agenda. Negotiators were barraged from all sides with an uncoordinated array of demands, deadlines, and threats. The deputy was tactically rescued after many hours of unproductive negotiations.

In a situation with multiple hostage takers without leadership or without a group decision-making process, the authorities will find themselves negotiating what amounts to several hostage situations simultaneously. While each of the hostage takers negotiates his own personal agenda, they are "sharing" the same hostage to enforce their demands. Any one of the hostage takers, individually, could take violent, aggressive action against a hostage for his own purposes, especially if he knew he would not be held personally responsible.

Finally, if the decision maker for hostage takers is outside the containment area, every effort should be made to isolate the contained hostage takers from their leadership. Isolation may be achieved by jamming radio frequencies, cutting telephone lines, or simply shutting off electricity. Negotiators want a leader to emerge from the contained group of hostage takers.

5. A Demand by the Hostage Taker

Hostage situations by definition involve substantive demands. If no substantive demands are made in an incident, it is not a hostage situation. Instead, the occurrence may be intended as a homicide, a homicide–suicide, an opportunity for sexual exploitation, or any number of other possibilities.

Barricaded offenders, even those holding innocent persons, for example, will often make nonsubstantive demands for such things as cigarettes, beer, a relative, pizza, and so forth. The negotiator should always ask him- or herself, "Is there an easier way to get the demand fulfilled?" If there is an easier way, what is the real purpose for holding the victims? There are any number of possibilities. The nature of the hostage taker's demands may provide a vital clue to the offender's mental state, personality, and motivation. The absence of substantive demands and/or escape demands, in particular, may be the first clue as to suicidal bent on the part of the hostage taker. The negotiators should be asking themselves, "If he does not want anything from us and he does not want to leave, what does he want out of this incident?"

6. Containment of the Hostage Taker

Some years ago, a law enforcement agency located a bank robber it had been after for some time because in the course of his robberies he had pistol-whipped a number of bank tellers and injured them quite severely. Upon locating the robber, the authorities telephoned his residence and demanded his surrender. The bank robber unsuccessfully attempted to escape through a back door, side window, and attic. Finally, he told his girlfriend, "Tell them I'm coming out and I'm coming out shooting!"

He did come out of the house but with a handgun to his own head, walking rapidly and shouting, "Get back! Get back! I'll kill myself!" The officers did stay back and attempted to keep him surrounded while maintaining their positions of cover by moving from car to tree to car down the street. The bank robber turned a corner, and officers had reason to believe that he entered a residence. The occupant of the residence was very fearful, and it took the officers twenty minutes to realize that she was afraid of them, not of anyone inside the house. The fugitive bank robber had escaped. Fortunately for the officers' careers, the bank robber surrendered himself the following day.

Containment in the smallest possible area is vitally important. Containment includes restraint from leaving the crime scene. In other words, there is no such thing as moving containment. If the offender and the incident are moving, the incident is not contained. Officials want to restrict the offender's movement, whether it be on foot or in a vehicle. Moving hostage incidents are often the most dangerous because they cause a loss of some measure of control, are difficult to command, and add problems in communication. The more officials can restrict the offender's freedom of movement, the better off negotiators are. He should have as little room as possible to move around, and the authorities should collapse perimeters around any areas he vacates, to deny him reentry. As the offender comes to see just how contained he is, he will realize that he cannot expect to harm or murder his victim with impunity.

7. Passage of Time

The passage of time in a hostage situation is often the best thing to happen for a negotiator because it does so much to accomplish a successful, nonviolent resolution. Time is so vitally important to achieving a successful resolution that the subject is worthy of a book by itself. Simply put, time provides the following advantages to the authorities:

1. The hostage taker's basic human needs, such as hunger and thirst, increase, and he comes to realize that only through the negotiator can his needs be met.
2. Anxiety diminishes.
3. As anxiety is reduced, the offender's ability to think more rationally increases.
4. A bond may develop between the hostage taker and his victim, thereby increasing the hostage's safety.
5. Opportunities for escape may arise for the hostages.
6. The gathering of information for good decision making takes place.
7. The formation of a negotiator/offender rapport may be established.
8. The offender's expectations are reduced.
9. The tactical team has an opportunity to formulate not only emergency and deliberate assault plans but also

plans for hostage releases, deliveries of items to the offender, and the offender's surrender.

On the negative side, time is expensive in terms of money and manpower. Exhaustion can lead to carelessness and irrational behavior on the part of law enforcement as well as the offender; blocking city streets for long periods of time can be inconvenient for large segments of the city's population and lead to pressure for a dangerous, immediate resolution to the situation. Injuries, illness, and the presence of drugs can also lead to demands for a quick solution. Nevertheless, time almost always works on the side of the authorities and against the hostage taker.

8. The Negotiator as a Significant Other

Law enforcement negotiators aim to establish a special relationship with the offender from the very beginning. They introduce themselves to the hostage taker by stating, "My name is _____ . I am a negotiator for the _____ Police Department, and I would like to help you work this out." Negotiators deliberately provide their name without rank to avoid the possibility that the offender may believe they have more power than they actually do. Also, introducing themselves as negotiators helps establish the appropriate relationship with the offender. As a representative of the police department, the negotiator does have access to power, even if he or she is not the final authority in the incident. As a negotiator, the official establishes that he or she can use this power to help or hurt the hostage taker. A significant other is someone who can hurt or help, and the negotiator has stated that he or she is willing to help. The negotiator appears to the offender not simply as a member of the enemy party but also as a possible ally in a difficult situation.

Summing Up Hostage Negotiation

Although hostage negotiators have enjoyed a remarkable record of success since the early 1970s, it is essential that negotiators understand *why* they are successful and, on the other hand, be able to readily recognize those circumstances under which the authorities *may not* be successful via negotiation. A thorough understanding of these eight elements will aid negotiators in determining the probability of success via negotiation, establishing negotiable circumstances, and maintaining a proud record of achievement.

KIDNAP NEGOTIATION: A TEAM EFFORT

The negotiation effort is far more than a team of negotiators talking to the "bad guy" over the telephone. What negotiators are saying to the offender is only part of the message being conveyed to him. In a sense, every crisis management component is part of the negotiation effort. The whole procedure includes not only what the negotiators say to the offender but also every observed move the tactical team makes, every radio and television broadcast the offender hears, and every decision made by management. For the negotiation effort to be maximally effective, all actions taken or not taken by each of the crisis components must communicate the same message. It is essential that all crisis management components follow the same strategy.

Planning Kidnap Negotiations

The crisis management team should meet early in the incident and regularly after that. Management must decide what message it wants to convey and how that message is to be conveyed. If management decides it wants to be tough, everybody is tough. Negotiators take a hard line. Tactical teams display an obvious presence. Management adopts a strong position that is reflected in their decisions and media releases. If management decides it wants to take a softer line, negotiators are more empathetic, the tactical teams maintain a low profile, and management is more conciliatory in its decision making. Management must make the overall decision on strategy, and each component of the team communicates management's message to the offender.

Periodically throughout the incident, the team members must meet to discuss progress, evaluate their strategy, and make adjustments as necessary. If the crisis management team shifts its strategy, everyone on the component teams must be informed of the change and briefed on what the new strategy is.

Expressing the same message to the offender obviously requires communication and agreement among all the crisis management components. If the components are not talking to each other and information is not passed down within their respective teams, it is unlikely that a single message will be communicated to the offender. What is required is not only *inter*team communication but also *intra*team communication. The actions of a single individual, if not in line with the current strategy, can destroy the efficacy of the negotiation effort and, perhaps, any chance of a peaceful resolution. Thus, management's giving negotiators full rein or allowing them to "do their thing" does little good unless the entire management team and the tactical team know what the negotiators are doing and support them by sending the same message to the offender. Differing messages from each component lead the offender to distrust the negotiators and believe that they have no influence with management, thus prolonging the incident or provoking an unwanted response.

For example, it is extremely difficult, if not impossible, for negotiators to convince the offender that the authorities intend him no harm when he can see tactical teams moving into position. Any movement by the tactical team while operating under this strategy must be accomplished with complete discretion. When the negotiators' strategy is to be reassuring, all the team's components must act accordingly, if they expect to appear credible to the offender.

Sometimes crisis managers deliberately abandon this policy of one message. Obviously, every critical incident is unique and requires a "game plan" of its own, just as each ball game is unique and requires its own game plan. Some offenders can be persuaded and coaxed, while others must be pressured to do the "right thing." When management decides to apply pressure, one sure way to do so is to inject uncertainty deliberately into the equation. An easy means of instilling uncertainty in an adversary's mind is to convey multiple, differing messages. His fear and paranoia will do the rest. Even in this situation, however, the type of differing message sent must be thought out beforehand, and each component must be aware of its role in the strategy. In a sense, every message communicated to the opposing side is part of the negotiation effort. Every person who conveys that message to the offender becomes part of the negotiation effort. Negotiators have tactical responsibilities such as the passing of intelligence information. Similarly, tactical team members have negotiation responsibilities in the message they convey to the offender. It is not enough to know and respect the role of the other crisis management components. It is essential that all components view themselves as part of a single, unified effort and convey only one message to the offender if the desired outcome is to be achieved.

Kidnap Negotiations in Foreign Settings

Nonpolitical hostage situations abroad most commonly involve either corporations or private families. When operating in foreign countries, especially underdeveloped countries, some United States corporations, rightly or wrongly, feel that it is necessary to "go it alone." Many reasons persist for this view. Often, the police are not adequately trained to handle the investigation and delicate negotiations that kidnappings require. Unfortunately, too, in many parts of the world corruption is rampant among the police and military. As a result, families and corporations are reluctant to trust them, sometimes with good reason. Finally, cultural differences make for uneasy feelings in the corporation or family.

Though corporate executives may have negotiated many business deals, a kidnap situation is usually unlike anything a businessperson has previously encountered. The stakes do not get much higher than in a kidnap situation, a situation that may affect the future course of a business in that country, the company's public image, morale, and sometimes its solvency. Emotion and stress, especially when the victim is known to the negotiation team, can weigh on the team's judgment to the point of affecting the outcome.

First, every effort should be undertaken to reduce the effects of stress. Planning and practicing the negotiation dialogue, having a third party who does not know the victim, or enlisting a panel of advisers composed of trusted friends, relatives, and experts are all steps that can avoid the negotiator's problems of stress and emotional involvement.

Unquestionably, negotiation experience—whether as a sales representative, labor negotiator, businessperson, or attorney—can be valuable experience to fall back on when negotiating with kidnappers. However, it should never be forgotten that the opposing team in a kidnapping situation is not composed of "typical" businesspeople. Some adversaries will suffer little from the burden of a conscience. They also may be impulsive, violent, and heavily armed; suffer from a wide variety of personality disorders; or be drug and alcohol abusers, career offenders, or fanatics.

Additionally, businesspeople are not normally concerned for the safety of their negotiator, but kidnap negotiations are not normal circumstances. Sometimes the safety of the family or corporate negotiator becomes a concern. Those events include any face-to-face negotiations, the ransom drop, recovery of the victim, and communication drops. Special care should be taken *at all times* when the offender knows that the extorted party is in possession of the money, whether the ransom be in the home, office, hotel room, or car.

Even though there may have been, in retrospect, hints of the coming crisis, kidnappings generally catch families and corporations by surprise. All good businesspeople do their homework before walking into a business negotiation, but a kidnap negotiation requires that the negotiation team play "catch-up," with a lot to do under very adverse conditions. Contingency planning for this unlikely event will go a long way toward reducing anxiety, stress, team hostility, and uncertainty, and such planning should be standard operating procedure for any company that does business in those parts of the world where such incidents are known to occur.

Kidnap or hostage negotiation should never be approached as an individual effort. The negotiator should be part of a team that provides ideas, emotional support, family or corporate consensus, information, and an opportunity to practice the negotiation. United States law enforcement negotiation teams have long successfully utilized the team approach, and a cardinal rule for them is to never negotiate alone.

The victimized group also needs to decide who will be representing them in the negotiation. The negotiator is often a family member, a law enforcement officer, a government or corporate official, a paid representative, a family friend, a clergyman, or an attorney. The advantages and disadvantages of each alternative are often situationally determined. Whoever is selected as negotiator should not represent him- or herself to the hostage taker as the ultimate decision maker. The negotiator should always say he or she must refer back to the rest of the family, corporate headquarters, Washington, D.C., downtown, or wherever decisions are being made. The negotiator should not refer to a single individual as the decision maker. The negotiator should position him- or herself as a conduit of information to the kidnappers, a mere spokesperson for the family or corporation.

Some family members have been excellent negotiators, but some obvious inherent problems are associated with their potential emotional involvement. Generally, it is best not to use a close family member, but, in a situation in which a suitable family member can maintain his or her composure and follow instructions, using family members can have several advantages. Their relationship to the victim provides immediate credibility that other parties might require time to develop. The kidnapper will tend to make certain assumptions because of the family relationship that the negotiation team may be able to use to its advantage. Also, family members know the victim well should that knowledge become important in a spontaneous, unanticipated development.

Other concerned persons and groups have their own objectives that may not readily align themselves with the negotiation team's objectives. Among others whose objectives may differ from the team's objectives are certain members of the victim's family, the police, the government, stockholders, unions, and media representatives. The objectives and priorities that emerge over time in a kidnapping crisis can be surprising, provoke anger, and have consequences lasting well beyond the resolution of the incident.

Objectives that may come into conflict with the negotiation team's objective of the victim's safe return include:

- Being able to continue business in the country when the kidnapping incident is over
- Maintaining corporate morale
- Preserving or enhancing the corporate public image
- Minimizing the amount of ransom paid
- Minimizing the victim's time in captivity
- Avoiding embarrassment to the corporation or other parties
- Identifying, apprehending, and prosecuting the offenders
- Attempting to deter future kidnappings
- Maintaining an inheritance
- Not "going public"
- Enhancing a personal position in the corporation, government, or family
- Being the first wire service or news network to break the story, have dramatic footage of the ransom drop, and so forth
- Maintaining the financial situation of the corporation or family

In some countries, using local law enforcement officers to negotiate or even notifying them of the incident may be a risky proposition. There may be problems of inexperience, cultural differences, possible corruption, and/or lack of training. In the

United States, however, the FBI has an excellent record in the successful resolution of kidnapping incidents.

A reluctance to negotiate and a desire on the part of families and corporations to pay the ransom immediately is not unusual. Bargaining for someone's life is an inherently nasty business, and no one wants to risk or bargain for the life of someone he or she cares about. Nevertheless, consider the following: if the ransom is paid immediately, the kidnapper may feel he seriously underestimated the wealth and resources of the family or corporation, decide not to release the hostage, and come back with a new, higher ransom demand. Such an outcome has happened.

Also, kidnappers are generally uncertain about how much they can get for the victim. If the family or corporation agrees to pay the demanded amount immediately, the kidnapper may conclude that they have no intention of paying and have notified the authorities. Most kidnappers *expect* to negotiate the ransom amount, and anytime a deviation from their expectations occurs, in any way, the risk to the victim increases.

The victim family or corporation often makes statements such as "We will do anything to get him [or her] back safely." These are very laudable feelings, but as a practical matter, the extorted parties cannot do anything to get the victim back; they have practical limits. Negotiators should not appear too eager or too willing to pay anything to get the victim back. The sooner the other side becomes convinced that the extorted party's financial limits have been reached, the sooner the situation will be resolved. Negotiators must be patient. They must be prepared and act prepared for a long siege. (In the United States, kidnappings for ransom rarely last more than a week or ten days. In other parts of the world, kidnappings lasting six months or more are common.)

In a kidnap for ransom, the kidnapper must communicate with the extorted party. The communication and demand generally take the form of telephone calls, tape recordings, or letters. Any telephone negotiation with the kidnappers should be tape recorded. Law enforcement hostage negotiators have found that tape recording the dialogue between hostage taker and the police can be useful not only for prosecution but also for the negotiation process, useful in that the tapes of the negotiation session can be reviewed for important negotiation hints that were lost in the "heat of battle." Everything the kidnappers say is a potentially helpful piece of information. Equally, however, every time the corporate or family negotiator is in contact with the kidnappers, the offenders are told far more than the spoken word. Care should be taken to ensure that the kidnappers are getting the message the team wants them to receive.

In negotiating the ransom amount, negotiators must be aware of the pattern of concessions in terms of amount and time. How much are the kidnappers coming down in their demanded amount, and how much is the extorted party going up in its counteroffer? Negotiators want the kidnappers to be coming down in significantly larger increments than the negotiators are going up. The extorted party should be going up in odd amounts and in progressively smaller increments. The family or corporation wants to give the impression to the kidnappers that they are being drained of every last dollar and there is just no more money.

The negotiation team should also look at the pattern of concessions over time. Who gains the most in terms of offers and counteroffers over time? Sometimes, kidnappers will not contact the extorted party for significant periods of time in an apparent attempt to pressure the family or corporation. Waiting, however, puts pressure on the kidnappers, too, because they do not know what the police, government, family, or corporation is doing. If the extorted party maintains its composure and comes back with only a minimal counteroffer after a significant amount of time has passed, the kidnappers will feel that the risk of the wait is not worth the marginal amount gained.

Perhaps the most difficult part of the negotiation process is talking the ransom down even further when the negotiator knows the ransom can be paid. As one family negotiator said, "The negotiation does not really begin until you get them down to a price you can pay." The fear that the victim may be killed when the ransom could have been paid is a very heavy burden for any negotiator to bear.

Negotiators should avoid expanding the pool of money available to pay the ransom—that is, they should not say anything to the kidnapper about borrowing money from friends, the bank, relatives, or the corporation. If the kidnappers tell the negotiator to go to the corporation, bank, relatives, and so on, for the money, the negotiator should say that corporate money is not available to pay ransoms, there is no collateral for a loan because the house was already mortgaged to meet the previous offer, and other members of the family and family friends are actually borrowers from the family and are in no position to provide money. The negotiation team does not want to give the impression that more money is "out there" if only the kidnappers are willing to risk the wait. In line with this, because of the risk involved in waiting for larger amounts, kidnappers may accept a much lesser sum than is available immediately. In response to a demand for money, the negotiators should consider telling the kidnappers that they will attempt to raise more money, but a smaller total is available *now.*

Negotiators should always insist on current evidence of a walking, talking victim. Polaroid photographs with the victim holding the day's newspaper is a common means of providing this evidence. Sometimes, the victim will read the day's front page on an audio- or videotape that is then sent to the family or corporation.

Naturally, all contacts with the kidnapper should be planned and rehearsed to the maximum extent possible. The more that developments are anticipated, the better prepared the negotiation team will be to counter them effectively. In anticipation of an incoming telephone call, for example, the negotiator should have a brainstorming, planning, and rehearsing session with the rest of the negotiation team. The negotiation team should role-play and ask "what if?" questions about every possible scenario they can dream up. The team should discuss possible responses and jointly decide on an appropriate response for every contingency. These rehearsals should include the give-and-take of the ransom negotiation itself; negotiator responses to violent and, perhaps, even gruesome threats; responses to unexpected threats, demands, or developments; and any other possible topics the negotiation team can conjure up. The team should decide not only what they will say but how they will say it. The negotiator should play his or her role in a "no holds barred" practice with the rest of the negotiation team.

Preparing for contact with the kidnappers will instill confidence in the negotiator, maximize the negotiation opportunity, help the negotiator maintain his or her composure, and reduce stress. A further objective of these brainstorming, planning, and rehearsal sessions is to avoid talking the team into a disadvantageous or possibly dangerous position with the kidnapper. If, when contact is made, a topic arises that has not been anticipated, discussed, and rehearsed, every effort should be made to delay discussion of that topic until the next negotiation session. Above all, negotiators must be patient. They must take their time and avoid the temptation to blindly agree to a proposition that has not been thought through by the negotiation team.

As mentioned in first-responder negotiations, lies and tricks are also to be avoided in kidnap negotiations. Tricks are to be avoided not because of any moral implications but because lies and tricks are difficult to keep going for long periods of time without getting caught. Lies are particularly difficult to maintain with changes in negotiator. It would not, for example, be a good idea to attempt to pass off a police officer as "Uncle Joe." We do not know with any certainty what the hostage is telling the kidnappers. Getting caught in a lie during a kidnap negotiation has the potential for being a lethal error.

Negotiators must be very careful about using humor in their contacts with the kidnappers. Negotiators do not want to create the impression that they are not taking the kidnappers or the negotiation seriously. Negotiators should bear in mind that the person they are dealing with is not just another businessperson. Moreover, joking is dangerous with mentally disturbed individuals and people with personality disorders. Negotiators can never be sure how the kidnapper will interpret the humor. Additionally, language and cultural problems make it very difficult to joke in a foreign language or through an interpreter, especially in a situation in which people are not expecting humor. If the kidnapper makes a joke and it seems appropriate for the negotiator to laugh with him, that response is all right. Negotiators, however, should not initiate the humor.

The negotiation team should not make any assumptions about their adversary. They must not underestimate the kidnappers, but, on the other hand, they should not give them undue credit, either. Sometimes their lack of preparation and planning is startling. The negotiating team, however, should be most careful of its actions and movements. There is a real possibility that negotiators will be watched, if only from time to time. They must avoid taking any actions the kidnappers could perceive as a threat.

As already mentioned, face-to-face negotiations with kidnappers are rare and should be strenuously avoided. If they are called for, however, the number one concern and priority is negotiation team safety. The team members should ask themselves why they are going face-to-face. What is to be gained in terms of the safe release of the victim? Does the benefit of this meeting outweigh the risk to the team? If the decision is to go face-to-face, the team must make sure that police will be covering the meeting, the negotiation site is one chosen by the team, and the meeting has been carefully planned. Again, the team should *not* accept the kidnapper's choice of site; it should select a different site. It should not walk into the offender's plan. Once the face-to-face plan is implemented, the team should not deviate from it in the slightest.

Parameters should be set for the meeting. Negotiators should state their limits before circumstances become confrontational. A negotiator might say, for example, "I'll tell you up front, my boss isn't going to let me [whatever the limits are], so don't even suggest anything like that because I'm not going to able to do it." It is better to get those kinds of issues out of the way before getting down to serious negotiations. The negotiator should also insist that no weapons be present, saying something such as, "I want to tell you up-front that my boss won't let me meet with you unless I'm assured that you won't be armed. He tells me he wants [the victim] back but not at the expense of losing me."

The objectives of the negotiation should be thoroughly discussed and priorities set. Most people agree that the safe return of the kidnap victim with minimal physical and/or psychological damage is the top priority and objective. A competing objective is the maintenance of the health and safety of the negotiation team itself. It is not helpful to the resolution of the crisis if a member of the negotiation team is killed, injured, or kidnapped.

CONCLUSION

First-responder negotiations, hostage negotiation, kidnap negotiation, and the resolution of other violent crises are best left to law enforcement officers who are trained, experienced, and paid to take the risks involved. However, time or other circumstances may demand that persons in the family, community, or corporation take action, if only a holding action, until help arrives. The action taken may be critical to the outcome of the crisis. Just as training is required to provide first aid in accidents, training is required to provide "first aid" in violent crises. We can go through life hoping we never happen upon an accident and never encounter violence, but neither eventuality is unlikely.

7

PSYCHOPHARMACOLOGICAL MANAGEMENT OF TRAUMATIC STRESS AND AGGRESSION

STUART B. KLEINMAN, M.D.

Violence in our society has serious implications for both victims and perpetrators. Although many approaches to managing both traumatic stress and aggressive behavior are possible, this chapter focuses on the specific approach of using psychopharmacological substances to manage traumatic stress and aggression. This approach has received increased attention but is not well understood. This chapter will provide a detailed overview of information not readily available.

Posttraumatic stress disorder is an anxiety disorder that, as defined in the textbook of psychiatric diagnosis, the *Diagnostic and Statistic Manual of Mental Disorders,* fourth edition *(DSM-IV),* may result from exposure to a traumatic event. This event must involve experiencing, witnessing, or being confronted with an extreme event that threatens death, serious injury, or the physical integrity of self or others. Moreover, the event must induce feelings of intense fear, helplessness, or horror. Interestingly, exposure to a traumatic event does not itself necessarily produce a posttraumatic stress disorder. Many individuals exposed to such an event do not develop this disorder. Whether an individual develops a posttraumatic stress disorder depends on the nature of the traumatic event, the nature of the individual's personality style (as of yet poorly defined), the individual's biological/genetic makeup, and the nature of the response of the individual's social network (e.g., family, friends, neighbors, town, country). The following discussion will concentrate on the one type of traumatic event that is on everyone's mind in our modern, urban society— violent crime.

FACTORS CONTRIBUTING TO POSTTRAUMATIC STRESS DISORDER

Several variables determine the degree of distress produced by a criminal victimization. These include the type of weapon, if any, used; the nature of threats, if any, made; the number of assailants; the nature of acts perpetrated; and the duration of the traumatic episode. One study of crime victims that compared the effects of adult sexual assault, robbery, and burglary found that it was rape and attempted rape that produced the greatest level of suicide attempts, suicidal ideation, and "nervous breakdowns" among the victims (Kirpatrick et al., 1985).

More important, the manner in which an individual perceives a life event largely determines its psychological effects. For example, an event perceived as non-life-threatening or lacking the possibility of serious physical injury or not experienced as uncontrollable will not produce a posttraumatic stress disorder. A potentially life-threatening situation that the victim believes can be safely overcome will likely not produce intense feelings of helplessness and fear. Without such an emotional "shock," a posttraumatic stress disorder will likely not develop.

Thus, individual differences in perception largely account for the varying responses to life events. Robbery by a knife-wielding teenager may be experienced in different ways. One individual may interpret the shaking hands of the youth as an indication of nervousness and may view the assailant's age as an indication of criminal inexperience. The victim may paternalistically view the assailant as a scared, wayward youth who represents no serious danger and so not feel terrified or helpless. Consequently, this individual would likely not develop a posttraumatic stress disorder.

On the other hand, another individual may view the assailant's shaking hands as a dangerous reflection of amateurism and may fear that the assailant will violently overreact. This victim may also believe that the assailant's youth signals special maliciousness and calculate that the attacker must be particularly vicious to engage in criminal activity at such a young age. As a result, this individual is terrified by the "mugger" and at high risk to suffer a posttraumatic stress disorder.

Previous trauma and the manner in which it was psychologically managed significantly impact an individual's response to current trauma. The age at which a trauma occurs further influences its effect. Prior experience of multiple traumas generally increases sensitivity to subsequent trauma. One study of individuals raised in crime-infested neighborhoods exposed to multiple traumas (e.g., those who had witnessed street violence) concluded that such individuals were at significant risk for developing a posttraumatic stress disorder (Breslau, Davis, Andreski, & Peterson, 1991). Repetitive childhood trauma, particularly within the context of a chaotic family system, may dispose an individual to the formation of a brittle psyche. Emotionally fragile individuals—for example, those with borderline personality disorder—are often unable to cope with intense feelings and are readily overwhelmed by the fear and rage generated by criminal victimization.

The quality of social support received after a traumatic event also strongly affects an individual's posttrauma psychological state. Unfortunately, nonvictims are often reminded of their vulnerability when in the proximity of crime victims. For instance, to avoid their own distress, nonvictim family members, friends, or colleagues may shun the trauma survivor, and they may also criticize the victim as a means of coping with their own discomfort. By labeling victims as wicked or foolhardy, nonvictims attempt to distance themselves from the victim, soothing their fear of victimization by subscribing to the myth that if only they act differently than the victim, then they will be safe. Nonvictims sometimes appear to act as if they will contract a "victim virus" if they come in contact with a crime victim. Even in those cases in which an individual's behavior may have actually heightened the risk of victimization, blaming the victim for the event still primarily serves the nonvictim rather than the victim.

This victim blaming typically magnifies an individual's distress by reinforcing the victim's already disturbing self-blame. The intensification of such feelings typically creates depression, and the shunning of crime victims, especially sexual assault victims, magnifies their feelings/fantasies of being damaged. Crime victims often interpret their exile from friends or family as a reflection of their undesirability. Ironically, social support is often lacking when it is needed most, further intensifying the stress.

Biological/genetic factors also influence whether an individual develops a posttraumatic stress disorder (Van der Kolk, 1988). An autonomic nervous system already highly reactive to environmental stimuli may predispose a victim to the physiological (physical) hyperactivity that characterizes posttraumatic stress disorder.

PRINCIPLES IN PRESCRIBING MEDICATION FOR POSTTRAUMATIC STRESS DISORDER

Treatment with medication should be considered if a posttraumatic stress disorder does not readily resolve or improve by itself. Posttraumatic stress disorder, as recognized by Abraham Kardiner in his work with World War I veterans, is a physioneurosis (Kardiner, 1941). Both psyche and soma (body) are disturbed in individuals suffering from such a condition. Individuals with a posttraumatic stress disorder have an impaired ability to control their physical reactions; even if they do not feel immediately fearful, their bodies may react as if danger is present.

Manifestations of posttraumatic physical disturbances include exaggerated startle reactions (e.g., jumping when a door closes); hypervigilance (e.g., assuming a tense, guarded posture outside the house); irritability; initial insomnia (difficulty falling asleep); and difficulty concentrating.

The behavior of a woman after being inadvertently shot in the neck during the robbery of a Korean grocery store exemplified post-traumatic irritability. A church-going, normally mild-mannered woman, she overreacted to minimal provocations by her live-in boyfriend. During mild disagreements, she would lose her temper and, for the first time, throw furniture at him. This behavior greatly embarrassed her.

No medication is currently available that cures posttraumatic stress disorder. The distorted threat assessment that characterizes this condition is relatively resistant to psychopharmacological intervention and requires psychological treatment, particularly cognitive therapy and risk assessment training. Medication is best utilized to target specific distressing symptoms. More than one medication may be necessary to address different symptoms. Medication may also enhance the beneficial effects of psychotherapy. The impaired bodily control produced by a posttraumatic stress disorder constantly reinforces the traumatized individual's distressing feelings of helplessness and depression. Diminished control over physical reactions may also trigger recollections of the lack of control experienced during the victimization. By increasing an individual's control over his or her body, medication may augment the traumatized individual's sense of autonomy and reduce anxious and depressive feelings.

Medication for Anxiety Symptoms

The anxiety components of a posttraumatic stress disorder may be treated with several medications. One of the most innocuous anxiety-reducing group of medications are beta-blockers. Beta-blockers, such as propranolol (Inderal), have long been used by physicians in the management of hypertension (high blood pressure), angina (heart-related chest pain), and cardiac arrhythmia (abnormal rhythm of the heart). These agents block peripheral (beta-adrenergic) cell receptors. Ordinarily, when these receptors are stimulated by adrenaline/norepinephrine, they produce anxiety (i.e., "fight or flight") reactions. By blocking the effects of adrenaline, beta-blockers reduce the physical manifestations of anxiety, such as increased heart rate. Such physical expressions of anxiety may be misinterpreted by an individual as a sign of serious impending injury, such as a heart attack or stroke, and cause that individual to become even more anxious, which bolsters the perception of impending doom and further magnifies anxiety. Medication, by literally blocking the physical signs of anxiety, interrupts this feedback loop and serves to decrease anxiety.

Beta-blockers, however, address only the peripheral signs of anxiety. They do not alter the fundamental physiological and psychological bases of anxiety. They do not influence the central nervous system (brain) pathways, the misperceptions of external events, or the distressing internal recollections that initiate anxiety. An individual may have distressing memories even if beta-blockers successfully inhibit physical signs of anxiety. Nevertheless, the safety and ease of use of beta-blockers promote their use, particularly among physicians less experienced in treating posttraumatic symptomatology.

Another antihypertensive agent that nonspecifically reduces anxiety is clonidine (Catapres). Unlike beta-blockers, which block peripheral (outside the central nervous system) receptors, clonidine directly stimulates the central nervous system's alpha II adrenergic receptors. Stimulation of these central receptors has the opposite effect of stimulation of peripheral beta receptors and decreases physical indicators of anxiety. Clonidine's anxiety-reducing effect is sometimes also used to aid detoxification from addictive drugs such as heroin. The main drawback to the use of clonidine stems from the fact that it induces low blood pressure (hypotension) and a consequent high blood pressure after it is stopped (rebound hypertension).

The benzodiazepines—diazepam (Valium), alprazolam (Xanax), and clonazepam (Klonopin)—are perhaps the most commonly used group of antianxiety agents. These medications more directly target anxiety than do beta-blockers or clonidine, by affecting the neurotransmitter GABA. The main disadvantage of their use is their potential to produce addiction. Substance abuse, particularly alcohol abuse, not infrequently accompanies posttraumatic stress disorder when individuals attempt to control their anxiety, depression, or rage via self-medication. Both alcohol and benzodiazepines depress the functioning of the central nervous system, but, in combination, they may also suppress respiration and in extreme cases produce a comatose state. An individual disposed to become addicted to alcohol is also disposed to become addicted to benzodiazepines. Thus, the prescription of benzodiazepines requires eliciting a careful substance abuse history and ongoing monitoring of usage.

Another drawback, albeit rare, to the use of benzodiazepines lies in their potential to trigger paradoxical rage reactions. Rather than create their usual sedating effect, they may cause agitation or anger. Short-acting benzodiazepines, which exert their effect for only limited periods (e.g., four to six hours), more commonly stimulate such reactions. Alprazolam and lorazepam (Ativan) are examples of commonly used short-acting benzodiazepines. Long-acting benzodiazepines, in contrast, remain in the body for extended periods, sometimes days with chronic use. Examples of long-acting benzodiazepines are diazepam and clonazepam. As posttraumatic stress disorder may increase the likelihood of violent acting out, particularly when it coexists with a personality and/or substance abuse disorder, benzodiazepines should be cautiously used. (Incidentally, a small subgroup of Vietnam combat veterans with posttraumatic stress disorder may be at special risk for addictive and violent behaviors.)

Another advantage of long-acting benzodiazepines is the relative ease with which they may be withdrawn. Long-acting benzodiazepines may not entirely leave the body for days after ingestion, and the slower benzodiazepines (or other drugs, for that matter) leave the body, the less severe the withdrawal reaction. The long-acting benzodiazepines, however, have the disadvantage of sometimes causing excessive sedation. Short-acting benzodiazepines permit more precise temporal control of anxiety symptoms. Ultimately, consideration of a patient's specific needs determines whether long- or short-acting benzodiazepines should be used.

Treatment of Panic Symptoms

Panic attack symptoms often accompany posttraumatic stress disorder. Panic attack symptoms include sudden onset of shortness of breath, chest pain, palpitations, lightheadedness, nausea, and intense fear of dying or of losing one's mind. These panic attacks typically occur suddenly and are relatively brief, usually fifteen to thirty minutes. Attacks may occur in response to specific stimuli associated with a traumatic event. For example, an individual mugged on a subway may experience panic attacks while on subways or while in other closed areas associated with transportation, such as buses. An individual assaulted at knifepoint may suffer panic attacks whenever exposed to dinner knives. A woman sexually assaulted by a tall bearded man may have panic attacks when exposed to similarly groomed men.

The tricyclic antidepressants imipramine (Tofranil) and desipramine (Norpramin) are usually effective in terminating panic attacks. These traditional antidepressants are known as tricyclics because of their three-ring chemical structures. They have been used for decades, and their side effects (which include sedation, dry mouth, difficulty in urinating, constipation, blurred vision, palpitations, lightheadedness upon rising, and weight gain) are well known. They may also induce cardiac arrhythmias, primarily in predisposed individuals. Desipramine tends to produce significantly fewer side effects than imipramine, its parent compound, and is generally well tolerated.

The monoamine oxidase inhibitor antidepressant phenelzine (Nardil) is also highly effective in treating panic attacks. Monoamine oxidase inhibitors are structurally distinct from tricyclic compounds and work in a different manner. They both, however, increase neurotransmitter function and are effective. Monoamine oxidase inhibi-tors may generate significantly elevated blood pressure, rarely even stroke, if combined with foods containing tyramine. Thus, monoamine oxidase inhibitors can only safely be used by individuals willing to avoid foods with significant amounts of tyramine. These include red wine, cured meats (e.g., bologna, salami), liver, pickled foods, smoked foods, and hard cheeses. The prohibition of foods containing hard cheeses, such as pizza, causes many to choose not to utilize this medication. A particularly common side effect of monoamine oxidase inhibitors is postural hypotension (i.e., low blood pressure upon rising to a sitting or standing position). Sexual dysfunction (e.g., anorgasmia), is infrequent but not rare. The side effects of tricyclic antidepressants and monoamine oxidase inhibitors are fully reversible with dose reduction or discontinuation.

High-potency benzodiazepines (e.g., clonazepam, alprazolam), exert specific antipanic effects independent of their general anxiety-reducing effects and are highly effective antipanic agents. Alprazolam and clonazepam are equally efficacious. Alprazolam is short acting; clonazepam is long acting. Whether other benzodiazepines also possess specific antipanic properties is not certain. In sufficiently high doses they may also be effective.

A woman who was repeatedly stabbed by a knife-wielding assailant greatly benefited from treatment with Clonazepam. The attack occurred while she was crossing the street after exiting a bus. She suddenly felt a sharp pain in her neck. As she was repeatedly stabbed she thought, "This is it," and believed she was going to die. She suffered serious physical injuries and might have died had not an individual passing by noticed her body slumped on the sidewalk and called Emergency Medical Services.

After recovering physically, the victim, for the first time in her life, started experiencing spontaneous panic attacks. She would suddenly feel shortness of breath and tightness in the chest and develop palpitations, sweats, and intense feelings of anxiety. She also became phobic of public transportation and certain streets/locales. Her panic attacks caused her great distress, and her aberrant behavior markedly impaired her functioning. Her perceptions of risk in her surroundings created anxiety and phobic behaviors. Typical of an individual who suffered a criminal victimization, she filtered subsequent events through the memory of the assault. She saw danger in relatively benign situations; the approach of a man on a crowded sidewalk in the middle of the day now frightened her.

Cognitive-behavioral therapy was utilized to treat her trauma-induced distorted risk assessment, and systematic desensitization was employed to decrease the anxiety associated with particular stimuli (e.g., streetlamps, bus shelters). Clonazepam was prescribed to treat her panic attacks and her generally heightened level of anxiety. Within approximately three weeks of beginning clonazepam, her panic attacks became significantly less severe and occurred less frequently. She began to feel calmer. After approximately six weeks of medication, her panic attacks virtually ceased. She continued on clonazepam for approximately six months while she received cognitive-behavioral treatment. Subsequently, the clonazepam dose was gradually reduced, and, after a four-week tapering period, it was fully discontinued. She experienced no withdrawal symptoms. Cognitive behavioral treatment was continued for another six months. By one year after a near-lethal attack, the victim was generally anxiety-free. She suffered only residual anxiety when exposed to certain reminders of the assault (e.g., the street where the attack had occurred).

Serotonin selective reuptake inhibitors (SSRIs) may be useful in the treatment of various posttraumatic stress symptomatology. These medications are often effective in reducing the obsessive thoughts that comprise obsessive compulsive disorder, and they may also reduce the frequency and intensity of recurrent, intrusive posttraumatic thoughts. Individuals with posttraumatic stress disorder often report that they cannot "turn off" their thoughts (and images) of the trauma. Serotonin selective reuptake inhibitors may facilitate increased control over such thoughts.

As they are often useful in the treatment of social phobia (e.g., irrational anxiety over eating or speaking in public, for fear of being humiliated), these inhibitors may also be useful in phobic avoidant symptoms. Individuals with posttraumatic stress disorder often become avoidant of people and places associated with the trauma, feeling that by avoiding reminders of the trauma, they may, at least temporarily, control their anxiety. Avoidance, however, is maladaptive when it interferes with an individual's ability to participate in usual life activities. Certain avoidant symptoms such as diminished interest in activities overlap depressive symptomatology. As effective antidepressants, SSRIs alleviate depressive-type posttraumatic stress symptomatology. By decreasing phobic avoidance, they may also indirectly reduce depressive symptoms by increasing access to social support. Isolation and diminished social support may secondarily produce or reinforce depressive feelings.

Serotonin selective reuptake inhibitors tend to render hypersensitive individuals less responsive to emotional stimuli. Depression triggered by hypersensitivity to rejection generally responds to this medication. Individuals receiving SSRIs also often report being less bothered by emotional lability ("mood swings"). Because posttraumatic stress disorder is characterized by physiological hyperreactivity, SSRIs may be reasonably expected to diminish environmental reactivity in individuals with this disorder.

The benefits of using serotonin selective reuptake inhibitors can be seen in the following case of a mother whose child was inexplicably murdered. Following the child's death, this woman experienced recurrent nightmares in which she visualized her son being shot. She was constantly bombarded by intrusive thoughts of her son's murder and became socially withdrawn, losing interest in most of her usual activities. She stopped driving and riding subways, she became irritable and developed difficulty falling asleep (i.e., initial insomnia), and she literally jumped when she heard loud noises (exaggerated startle reaction). Initially, she was treated with individual and group therapy. Although her condition stabilized, she continued to experience significant posttraumatic and depressive symptomatology. Subsequently, she sought a psychiatric consultation, and the SSRI fluoxetine (Prozac) was added. Within two weeks, the frequency and intensity of intrusive thoughts diminished, depressive feelings diminished, and irritability decreased. Over a period of several weeks, the dose of fluoxetine was increased. By eight weeks after beginning treatment with this medication, the quality of this woman's life had greatly improved. She continued to grieve the sudden death of her son and to be angry at "the system." However, she had nightmares less frequently, was more social, tolerated others better, and was less hyperreactive to environmental stimuli. She experienced no side effects and was pleased with fluoxetine's results.

TREATMENT OF AGGRESSION

Aggressive behavior is defined by Bond (1992) as behavior intended to harm another. When such behavior is not an appropriate response to a provocation, it may be considered pathological. Pathological aggression is a consequence of intrapsychic and extrapsychic factors. Extrapsychic contributors include social, cultural, and economic forces. Alteration of these forces may diminish or heighten an individual's propensity toward acting violently. Intrapsychic contributors include psychological forces.

Understanding Aggression

Much of the current state of understanding of aggression derives from animal studies. The forms of aggression identified in animals (Valzelli, 1981) include:

1. predatory,
2. competitive,
3. defensive,

4. irritative,
5. territorial,
6. maternal protective,
7. female social,
8. sex related, and
9. instrumental.

Valzelli reports that these forms of aggression represent mechanisms for self- and species preservation. Each form of aggression may have a different neurophysiological substrate (Moyer, 1971). Consequently, a "specific" and "universal" antiaggression drug may not exist (Valzelli, 1988).

Brain stimulation and ablation (destruction of a particular brain area) studies indicate that the limbic system of the brain is integrally involved in aggressive behavior (Wishik et al., 1989). The limbic system includes parts of the cortex (orbitomedial and orbitopolar frontal cortex), components of the cerebral hemispheres (hippocampus, amygdala, nuclei of the thalamus and hypothalamus), and areas of the midbrain. The limbic system coordinates information regarding the external environment, which is processed by the cortex, and information concerning the inner environment (e.g., hormone levels), which is processed by the hypothalamus. It also plays an important role in learning, memory, sexual behavior, and emotional responses. Multiple interconnections among components of this system render it unlikely that specific behaviors are simplistically localized to particular parts of the brain.

Multiple neurotransmitters (chemicals that transmit messages in the nervous system), including serotonin, norepinephrine, and dopamine, have been implicated in producing spontaneous aggression in animals. No single neurotransmitter likely solely accounts for aggressive behavior (Valzelli, 1984). Laboratory studies of animals, however, repeatedly implicate serotonin as a major contributor to aggressive behavior.

Decreased inhibitory control by the serotonergic system may be a common point in the expression of aggression in humans (Fishbein, Zovsky, & Jaffe, 1989). Changes in the metabolism of serotonin have been found in individuals who have been violent to themselves or others (Van Praag, 1989). Decreased cerebrospinal fluid 5-hydroxy indoleacetic acid (5-HIAA) has been associated with aggressive behavior (Kruesi et al., 1990; Morand & Young, 1983). Depletion of the amino acid tryptophan, a precursor to the production of serotonin, was shown in one study to be associated with increased impulsiveness. Male subjects deprived of dietary tryptophan were significantly more "angry," "aggressive," "annoyed," "quarrelsome," and "discontented" than those given a mixture of amino acids containing tryptophan (Cleare & Bond, 1994).

Causes of Aggressive Behavior

Aggressive behavior has multiple, treatable neurological causes. Normal-pressure hydrocephalus (increased fluid in the brain), typically associated with dementia, gait instability, and urinary incontinence, may also be present with unexplained agitation and aggression. Slowly increasing intracranial (within the skull) pressure from sources such as a stroke or tumor may produce increased agitation in the absence of other symptomatology. Metabolic encephalopathy (brain malfunctioning) is a frequent cause of agitation. One man whom I examined committed murder while in a psychotic, hyponatremic (pathologically low-salt) state. This individual most likely suffered from the syndrome of psychosis, intermittent hyponatremia, and polydipsia (excessive ingestion of water). Besides salt imbalance, other causes of metabolic encephalopathy include hidden infection, kidney failure, liver failure, heart failure, hypoxia (oxygen deprivation), and vitamin insufficiency (Wishik et al., 1989).

Seizure disorders are controversially linked to aggressive behavior. Such behavior may occur during, immediately following, or between seizures. Actual violence is rare, brief, and in almost all cases nonpurposeful, as would be expected from disjointed firing of nerve cells (Blumer & Benson, 1982; Delgado Escueta et al., 1981). Complex-partial seizures associated with temporal lobe dysfunction may include the performance of complex automatic behaviors, and it has been argued that this form of epilepsy is responsible for violent acts (Devinsky & Bear, 1984; Leicester, 1982; Monroe, 1985). However, the commission of related profit-motivated violence such as robbery would likely never occur.

Temporal lobe dysfunction may be associated with heightened emotional reactivity and aggressive and inappropriate behavior. A conglomeration of personality characteristics associated with temporal lobe abnormality has been described as Geschwind syndrome (Wishik et al., 1989). Features of Geschwind syndrome include emotional volatility, intense humorless style, hypergraphia (excessive writing), hyposexuality, and hyperreligiosity.

Another biological cause of violent behavior may be traumatic brain injury. Damage to the prefrontal lobes of the brain may produce disinhibited or impulsive behavior, labile or inappropriate affect, impaired judgment, and poor insight (Cummings, 1985). In response, for example, to a verbal insult, such individuals may experience exaggerated rage. Damage to the frontal lobe may also contribute to aggressive behavior in some cases of mental retardation. In one study (Damasio et al., 1990), sociopathic individuals with bifrontal lobe damage were found to have decreased skin conductance (sweating), a response to stimuli generally associated with anxiety. Abnormal physiological signs of anxiety (e.g., decreased sweating) have been cited as contributors to the sociopath's diminished sense of guilt and lack of self-control.

An example of aggression caused by brain impairment was the erratic behavior of a sixty-year-old, highly successful businessman. This man impulsively touched the breast (over her clothing) of a female employee. He had never before acted violently or sexually or been arrested. He had emigrated to the United States and, via hard work and good judgment, had become wealthy. Over the course of several months prior to the assault, this man became increasingly withdrawn and irritable and complained of having memory problems for the first time in his life. Psychiatric examination revealed suspicious thinking, difficulty performing relatively simple calculations, and impaired learning ability. These deficiencies were grossly inconsistent with his history of success as a financial investor. He was likely slowly developing dementia. Personality changes, such as irritability and suspiciousness, are frequently a characteristic of dementia.

Although Alzheimer's disease, which is not curable, is the most common cause of dementia, several other causes are possible, many of which are treatable and fully reversible.

Another biological cause of violent behavior is substance abuse. Alcohol alone or in conjunction with psychosis increases the likelihood of such behavior (Holcomb & Anderson, 1983; Swanson et al., 1990). A sedative, alcohol may induce violence via its disinhibitory effect. Under the influence of alcohol individuals may think thoughts they would not ordinarily think or act out impulses they would ordinarily restrain. Stimulants such as cocaine and amphetamines may also induce violence. Cocaine intoxication produces irritability, agitation, and suspiciousness, characteristics linked to violence. Chronic stimulant use may produce a paranoid delusional disorder and violence. Maniclike delirium and violence may also be produced. Intense craving for crack, in combination with chemically based impulsiveness, likely contributed to the increased number of robberies during the crack epidemic of the 1980s.

Phencyclidine (PCP) is generally recognized to be associated with severe violence. Unlike, for example, LSD, PCP is not a hallucinogen or a psychedelic drug. It is a dissociative anaesthetic that impairs the ability to sense and assess stimuli (Fauman & Fauman, 1982). Violence associated with PCP may be spasmodic and the product of impulsiveness and diminished reality testing. Bizarre acts associated with blatant psychosis, apparent increased strength, and unresponsiveness to external stimuli (e.g., police commands), may occur.

Psychosis may be associated with violent behavior (Tardiff, 1992; Taylor & Gunn, 1984). Individuals with paranoid schizophrenia may respond to delusionally perceived threats in a violent fashion. Hallucinations commanding an individual to commit violent acts, particularly if the hallucinations threaten the afflicted individual with harm if the command(s) are not obeyed, may also trigger violent behavior. In legal settings an individual may falsely report the presence of a command hallucination to bolster an "insanity defense." Conversely, an individual may falsely report the absence of such a hallucination to gain release from a locked psychiatric ward.

Individuals with paranoid schizophrenia, as compared with individuals with other forms of schizophrenia, tend to be especially dangerous because their cognitive ability often remains (relatively) intact. For example, in response to a paranoid delusion, an individual may carefully plan his or her mode of "defense." This "defense" may include acquiring and training with a weapon. Manic patients, in contrast, typically are violent as a function of their excitability, poor impulse control, and mood swings (Yesavage, 1983). An acutely manic individual is more likely to suddenly explode violently, particularly in response to limit setting, than he or she is to organize and plan a violent "defense" to a perceived threat.

Borderline and antisocial personality disorders are also associated with an increased risk of violence (Craig, 1982). Individuals with borderline personality disorder are disposed to outbursts of rage, impaired insight, poor judgment, mood swings, and destructive wishes. Individuals with antisocial personality disorder may be disposed to harm others because of deficient empathic ability and faulty self-restraining mechanisms (i.e., guilt). Quasi-delusional (grandiose) beliefs that legal authorities are readily outwitted and (narcissistic) gratification from taking advantage of this (i.e., the pleasure of "putting one over") also contribute to the commission of violence by individuals with antisocial personality disorder.

Attention deficit hyperactivity disorder (ADHD) is a risk factor for the development of childhood conduct disorder and adult antisocial personality disorder (Wishik, Bachman, & Beitsch, 1989). Features of ADHD include impulsiveness, episodes of rage, mood lability, and stress intolerance. Associated "soft" neurological signs (i.e., nonspecific neurological findings) include poor visuomotor coordination, hypersensitivity to sound, exaggerated startle reactions, poor eye tracking, and reflex abnormalities. Underactivity of the frontal (brain) lobes and associated diminished inhibitory control over lower (more primitive) brain centers may contribute to the behavioral difficulties of those with ADHD (Damasio, Tranel, & Damasio, 1990). Most adults with ADHD and without an accompanying antisocial personality disorder are nonviolent.

Treatment of Aggressive Behavior

No one drug effectively treats all forms of aggression because aggres-sion takes many forms. Impulsive violent behavior associated with borderline personality disorder, for example, is quite different from planned murder by an antisocial contract killer. One means of conceptualizing aggression for purposes of treatment is to view it as a consequence of stimulus (input) overload coupled with dysregulation (abnormality) of cognition, attention, mood, and/or arousal (Ratey & Gordon, 1993). Such stimulus overload may be produced by either external or internal factors.

Impaired cognition may dispose individuals to anger by limiting their ability to process and organize stimuli—a faulty information filter somewhere is hindering the correct assessment of incoming data. Consequently, individuals with this problem may often feel confused, frustrated, and overwhelmed by stimuli from within and without. One class of medication that helps people improve information processing is composed of the neuroleptics, which include the phenothiazines (e.g., Thorazine) and the butyrophenones (e.g., Haldol). Neuroleptics are a reasonable treatment choice for psychotic individuals with impaired information processing and distorted perceptions, and they are commonly employed for managing aggressive behavior.

The side effects of neuroleptics, however, include sedation, blood pressure changes, blurred vision, dry mouth, constipation, inhibited urination, and tachycardia (increased heart rate), which make the use of this class of drugs less than ideal. These effects typically occur initially, at higher doses and with low-potency agents (e.g., Thorazine). Disturbing dystonic reactions and pseudoparkinsonism are not uncommon with high-potency agents such as Haldol. Dystonic reactions are intense, involuntary muscular contractions that may produce contortion of the face and neck. They are readily reversed with appropriate treatment such as intramuscular diphenhydramine (Benadryl) or benztropine (Cogentin). Pseudo-parkinsonism symptoms include shuffling gait, slowed movement, and rigidity. This phenomenon is usually quite responsive to benztropine as well as to dopamine-enhancing medication such as amantadine (Symmetrel).

Chronic use of traditional antipsychotic agents, presumably due to dopamine-blocking effects (and associated receptor super-sensitivity), may produce tardive dyskinesia (manifested by involuntary writhing muscle movements that may be irreversible). This phenomenon occurs in approximately 20 percent of chronically exposed individuals (Kleinman, 1990), and no reliably effective treatment for it is presently available.

One potential side effect of traditional antipsychotic medication, the subjective feeling of motor (and mental) restlessness known as akathisia, may induce intolerable tension and precipitate aggressive behavior (Ratey, Sorgi, & Polakoff, 1985). Akathisia may be controlled or reduced by propranolol or lorazepam or eliminated by reduction of the neuroleptic dose.

Aggression associated with attention deficits may be successfully treated with psychostimulants such as dextroamphetamine (Dexedrine) and methylphenidate (Ritalin). These medications have been demonstrated to diminish impulsive behavior by enhancing attention and reducing hyperactivity. Ritalin has been shown to increase self-control (Hinshaw, Buhrmester, & Heller, 1989a), decrease inattention (Kaplan et al., 1990), and diminish verbal and physical aggression in boys with ADHD (Hinshaw et al., 1989b). Psychostimulants may also benefit head injury patients with impaired arousal and attention. The prescription of psychostimulants must always involve monitoring of blood pressure and pulse. Also, amphetamines have significant abuse potential; thus, patients must be watched for signs of inappropriate usage.

Another treatment for ADHD is tricyclic antidepressants, particularly desipramine. These drugs have been reported to be effective in 40 percent of adults with attention deficits. Desipramine may reduce the impulsiveness, tantrums, and mood shifts of ADHD that trigger aggression (Huessy, 1992).

Stabilization of mood, particularly during acute manic episodes, may also help prevent or control aggression. Lithium remains the most commonly utilized "mood stabilizer," and it has proved useful as an antiaggressive agent in emotionally labile individuals who are hypersensitive to stimuli (Mattes, 1986). In addition to regulating mood, lithium may reduce aggression in incarcerated felons without causing global sedation or inhibition (Marini & Sheard, 1977). Lithium may also reduce aggression in hyperactive children (Campbell, Perry, & Green, 1984), premenstrual women, individuals with personality disorders (Ratey, Gutheil, & Leveroni, 1991), and individuals with organic brain syndrome (Glenn et al., 1989). Irritability (and dissociative reactions) may produce violent outbursts by individuals with posttraumatic stress disorder, and lithium has also been reported to decrease such irritability (Forster, Schoenfeld, Marmar, & Lang, 1995).

Side effects (dose related) of lithium include nausea, vomiting, diarrhea, tremor, short-term memory difficulties, increased frequency of urination, and excessive drinking of water. Chronic use may cause hypothyroidism (low thyroid functioning). Kidney functioning should be monitored, although renal damage, if it occurs, is rare.

Lithium was quite effective in treating a twenty-year-old college student who, while in the midst of an acute manic episode, was excitable and agitated. During a conversation with a friend, he threatened to "pull the trigger." Over a period of weeks this individual had become increasingly grandiose, overproductive (remaining awake long into the night devising plans for world peace), and alternately irritable and euphoric. He was involuntarily hospitalized after yelling and screaming irrationally in his dormitory room. He was initially treated with clonazepam, which tranquilized him. Subsequently, lithium was added, and his grandiosity and excitation decreased. Eventually, clonazepam was discontinued, and he remained only on lithium. His mood returned to normal, and after missing a semester of school, he returned to campus where he performed well.

Hyperarousal may impair an individual's adaptive ability (Van der Kolk & Greenberg, 1987) and predispose toward aggressive behavior (Ratey, Sands, & O'Driscoll, 1986). Excessive firing of the sympathetic nervous system in response to external or internal stimuli is a cause of hyperarousal; and psychotic, developmentally disabled, or brain-injured individuals can experience internally confusing and perhaps excessive inner stimuli that produce hyperarousal and diminished frustration tolerance. Repetitive inner arousal has been hypothesized to sensitize an individual to environmental stimuli and produce a state of chronic "overload." Consequently, even a relatively minimal psychosocial stressor may kindle abnormal firing of brain cells and induce an excessive behavioral response. Behaviors that were initially triggered by a stressor may subsequently occur spontaneously (Ratey & Gordon, 1993).

The use of beta-blockers may decrease arousal by decreasing certain nervous system activity. Reduction of hyperarousal may produce improvement in learning, memory, and performance as well as overall enhanced cognitive functioning (Ratey & Lindem, 1991). Beta-blockers have successfully reduced aggressive behavior in individuals with intermittent explosive disorder (Granville-Grossman & Turner, 1966), conduct disorder (Williams, Mehl, & Yudofsky, 1982), dementia, (Greendyke et al., 1986), organic brain injury, developmental disabilities (Greendyke & Kanter,

1986), and chronic schizophrenia (Yudofsky, Silver, & Schneider, 1987).

Conditions indicating that beta-blockers should not be used include bronchial asthma, congestive heart failure, sinus bradycardia (slowed heart rhythm), and Raynaud's disease. As hypotension and bradycardia may occur, particularly at high doses, pulse and blood pressure should be monitored when beta-blockers are prescribed.

Decreased arousal may also be achieved by raising cerebrospinal fluid serotonin levels. Fluvoxamine (Luvox), a serotonin selective reuptake inhibitor, has been demonstrated to nonspecifically decrease aggression (Coccaro et al., 1989). Fluoxetine (Prozac) may be useful in treating organically impaired agitated patients (Sobin et al., 1989), impulsive aggression in patients with severe personality disorders (Coccaro et al., 1990), and impulsive and depressive symptoms in individuals with borderline personality disorder (Cornelius et al., 1990). Both lithium and fluoxetine have been used to reduce irritability in veterans with posttraumatic stress disorder (Shay, 1992). The side effects of SSRIs include gastrointestinal distress, fatigue, restlessness, weight loss, insomnia, diminished libido and sexual dysfunction.

The serotonin potentiator and antianxiety agent buspirone (BuSpar) may reduce aggressiveness associated with overarousal (Huessy, 1992). Specific patient groups for which buspirone has diminished violent behavior include individuals with dementia (Colenda, 1988), developmentally disturbed individuals (Ratey et al., 1989), and brain-injured individuals (Levine, 1988). Buspirone may also reduce aggression associated with severe premenstrual irritability (Rickels, Freeman, & Sondheimer, 1989). Individuals typically readily tolerate buspirone. Unlike other antianxiety medications, buspirone does not induce dependence and does not cause sedation. Common side effects include nausea, headaches, and lightheadedness. Toxicity is rare.

Another group of serotonergic agonists (5-HT_{1A} and 5-HT_{1B} [receptor] agonists) currently being researched comprises the "serenics" (Olivier et al., 1990). This group of agents, which include etoprazine, holds great promise. Preliminarily, the serenics appear to diminish "pathological" but not "nonpathological" aggression. In animals, they have reduced offensive aggression without diminishing appropriate defensive behavior. Serenics appear to exert antiaggressive effects without producing sedation, muscle relaxation, or inhibition of social interest or activity. In healthy humans, this drug has been safe and well tolerated (De Koning et al., 1991).

The atypical antipsychotic agent clozapine (Clozaril) may also be an effective antiaggressive agent (Ratey & Gordon, 1993). In one study (Ratey et al., 1993), the addition of clozapine to patients' already existing drug regimens produced significant reduction in aggressive behavior that, in some instances, was independent of reduction of psychosis. Assaults decreased by 31.8 percent, self-abusive behavior by 36.5 percent, agitation and verbal aggression by 48.5 percent, time in seclusion by 22.2 percent, and, significantly, time in restraints by 78.6 percent.

The most problematic potential adverse effect of clozapine is agranulocytosis (depletion of white blood cells) and the associated risk of serious infection. Consequently, regular blood monitoring is required. This drug is particularly indicated for treatment resistant schizophrenia, particularly resistant negative symptoms, and schizophrenia accompanied by tardive dyskinesia. Clozapine is unique (with the possible exception of risperidone [Risperidol]) among antipsychotic agents in not producing tardive dyskinesia. Several additional antipsychotic drugs with the utility of clozapine but without its side effects will likely be available soon.

Anticonvulsants, especially carbamazepine (Tegretol), have also been used effectively to reduce aggression (Yesavage, 1983). Tegretol has successfully treated intermittent episodic dyscontrol syndrome (a controversial diagnostic entity) and aggression associated with borderline personality disorder and schizophrenia (Bond, 1992). Its primary behavioral effects are reduction of overactivity, aggression, and poor impulse control (Elphick, 1989). Drawbacks to its use include potential production of agranulocytosis, severe exfoliative (skin-losing) rash, and liver abnormalities. Blood monitoring is, therefore, a condition for its use. Another anticonvulsant that may be used is valproate (Depakote). Problematic side effects include sedation and liver abnormalities.

Carbamazepine was useful in diminishing the aggressive behavior of an individual hospitalized in a forensic psychiatric facility. He had attacked several individuals on the hospital ward, including a staff member, in response to minimal provocation. This individual had a "pathological temper" and was impaired in his ability to control his impulses. His violent behavior posed a danger to others and himself. On one occasion he was punched in the head by another patient during a retaliatory attack.

Carbamazepine was prescribed to control his impulsiveness. The dose was gradually increased, and his white blood cell count was regularly monitored. Over the course of approximately six weeks, he became significantly less irritable and impulsive. When angered, he was less disposed to act out violently. He was more apt to scream rather than to strike. He also sought staff assistance more often. His white blood cell count remained within a safe range during the course of treatment.

Sedatives, particularly benzodiazepines, may reduce aggression (Corrigan, Yudofsky, & Silver, 1993). However, chronic use of these drugs may produce dependency, confusion, or intensification of depression, and, as previously noted, on rare occasions paradoxical rage reactions may also occur (Bond & Lader, 1979; Dietch & Jennings, 1988). Sedatives are best used to calm acutely agitated individuals.

Pharmacological treatment of sexual aggression typically involves the use of the antiandrogens (antimale hormones), including medroxyprogesterone acetate (MPA) or cyproterone acetate (Itil & Reisberg, 1978). Intramuscular MPA every seven to ten days has been shown to diminish sexual arousal and response in men (Blumer & Migeon, 1975). Cyproterone acetate also has been demonstrated to treat repetitively sexually aggressive men effectively (Money, 1970).

Medicolegal Issues

Although the drugs reviewed here are effective and safe to various degrees in reducing aggressive behavior, they are not officially approved by the Food and Drug Administration (FDA) for this purpose. The *Physicians Desk Reference* (PDR) will not, therefore, list treatment of aggressive behavior as a specific indication for use of these agents. However, prescription of these drugs for violent behavior is not prohibited by the Food, Drug and Cosmetic Acts. The act states, "Once the new drug is in a pharmacy, the physician may, as part of the practice of medicine, lawfully prescribe a different dosage for his patient, or may otherwise vary the conditions of use from those approved in the package insert, without informing or obtaining approval of the Food and Drug Administration." (*FDA Drug Bulletin,* 1971).

Despite the language of the act, a bad outcome may trigger a lawsuit. To prevail, a plaintiff must demonstrate that treatment fell below the standard of care. In such a suit, a plaintiff will typically argue that an agent was prescribed inappropriately, citing the PDR as support of this allegation. Expert testimony regarding the state of the art of treatment of aggression, in conjunction with a review of current (relevant) medical literature, more accurately establishes standard and reasonable pharmacological means of treating aggressive behavior.

Obtaining informed consent for using antiaggression agents is both good medical and good legal practice. Obtaining such consent, however, does not necessarily require formalistic procedures such as consent forms. Informed consent consists of three components: (1) information, (2) competency, and (3) voluntariness. An individual should be provided with information that a reasonable person would want in deciding whether to accept or reject treatment. Consent can only be given if an individual is competent to weigh risks, benefits, and alternatives rationally, and if treatment is not coerced. For example, granting increased hospital privileges or release from the hospital in exchange for acceptance of antiaggression medication may be potentially coercive.

Conclusion of Medical Treatment of Aggression

No single, reliably efficacious pharmacological agent for the treatment of aggressive behavior now exists, and the multiple causes of aggression make the development of such an agent in the near future unlikely. Situational variables (e.g., interpersonal conflict), environmental circumstances (e.g., crowded living circumstances), intrapsychic dynamics (e.g., diminished self-esteem), and biological factors (e.g., frontal brain damage) may all contribute to provoking violent behavior. Treatment should address those variables most relevant to an individual's aggressive behavior. For example, propranolol may be effective for organically (e.g., brain damage) based violent behavior, whereas carbemazepine may prove especially useful for interpersonally triggered impulsiveness associated with borderline personality disorder.

Agents that affect serotonergic transmission possess significant potential for improving the treatment of aggressive behavior. Targeting specific serotonin receptors linked to aggressive behavior may increase treatment utility and decrease side effects. The use of serenics reflects this strategy (Kravtiz & Fawcett, 1994).

Despite the recent advances in the psychopharmacological management of aggression, frequently several antiaggression agents must be tried before one that is both effective and tolerated can be found.

8

MEDIA DEPICTION AND COVERAGE OF VIOLENCE

The Impact on Family and Community

ELIZABETH K. CARLL, Ph.D.

The media have always covered violence, but recent years have seen a virtual bombardment of news stories recounting murder, rape, assault, and other atrocities. The O. J. Simpson trial on television had the entire nation tuning in and drew ratings surpassing the most popular soaps. Susan Smith's murder of her children was the headline story on the evening news for several weeks. Unfortunately, the media not only reflect what is occurring in our society but also reinforce stereotypes of how women are portrayed, both as victims and perpetrators of violence. *How* the news media cover violent incidents involving women is, therefore, vitally important because the media play such a major role in shaping public opinion and policy, to say nothing of their influence on the way children perceive the world (Carll, 1994).

The media have certainly found much material to work with in its coverage of violence involving women. The study *Rape in*

159

America: A Report to the Nation (Crime Victims Research and Treatment Center, 1992) concludes that 1.3 women are raped every minute in this country. According to the U.S. Department of Justice (1993), 4,936 women were murdered in 1992.

THE MEDIA'S STEREOTYPE OF WOMEN AS VICTIMS OF VIOLENCE

The stories concerning rape and violence against women certainly reinforce the rather commonly held notion that such crimes are in some way less significant than other forms of violence. For example, on February 12, 1994, the police arrived at Jennifer Galloway's apartment building in Queens, New York, and found her bleeding from twelve stab wounds to her face, neck, throat, and head. Before being stabbed, Singh, her ex-boyfriend, who was arrested at the scene of the crime, hit her on the head with a four-pound piece of cable. Police found three knives covered in blood. A fourth knife was found bent and sticking out of her head when she made it to a neighbor's apartment to get help. She stated that he was in a rage because she was about to become engaged to another man. He claimed self-defense, saying she was in a rage because he would not marry her. He had one small cut between his fingers. During the course of the trial, insinuations were introduced that made Galloway appear to be a run-around. In May 1995, Singh was cleared of all charges in the stabbing attack on Galloway, but—even more chilling—was the comment by one of the jurors after the verdict: "Hey, men and women fight." After the verdict, Galloway commented, "If it had been a stranger who did this, he'd be in jail. But in 1995, we're still considered men's property" (Stasi, 1995). Five similar newspaper stories of violence against women were also briefly reported in 1995 (Furse, 1995).

This epidemic of violence against women is especially worrisome because the majority of women who are victims of violence are raped, assaulted, and murdered by men they know. Given the dismissive attitude of the previously quoted juror, we can see that if a woman has the misfortune to know her attacker, the crime is seen by the public as a "misdemeanor" murder or rape. I use this term to illustrate that such crimes are not considered as serious as other forms of violence that people commit against each other.

The stereotyped media portrayals of women as victims or perpetrators not only influence the court of public opinion but, unfortunately, also become embedded in our justice system. Imagine a judge ordering a woman who was abused by her boyfriend to marry him. In a July 15, 1995, Associated Press report, a Cincinnati judge ordered a man, who pleaded no contest to having punched his girlfriend in the mouth, to marry her within nine months or risk being jailed. "I happen to believe in traditional American values," stated Municipal Court Judge Albert Mestemaker. The judge said that he wrote the requirement (even though he knew it would not stand up legally) after he learned that the couple had been living together for five years and had a five-year-old daughter.

In another case, in February 1994, a Maryland man, Peacock, shot and killed his wife because she was unfaithful. The judge imposed the minimum sentence of eighteen months' jail time for the murder and was reported to have stated, "I seriously wonder how many men married five, four years would have the strength to walk away without inflicting some corporal punishment. . . . I am forced to impose a sentence . . . only because I must do it to keep the system honest." The latter incident was covered only by one short wire service story that was printed nondescriptly in some newspapers (Associated Press, October 19, 1994). Perhaps what is really noteworthy here is that this decision resulted in a number of discussions on radio talk shows and also an article in the *Washington Post* (Rosenfeld, 1994), highlighting the public outrage over the inappropriate sentence of eighteen months with possible work release. The article stated that within two weeks of the sentencing, Peacock was placed in a work-release program at a trucking company from 5 A.M. to 9 P.M. As reflected by public reaction, it would appear that perception of the gravity of domestic violence is only now slowly beginning to change.

THE MEDIA'S STEREOTYPE OF WOMEN AS PERPETRATORS OF VIOLENCE

Violence against women and crimes of passion by men have a long record in history and cultural tolerance (see Chapter 3). These "misdemeanor" murders and assaults rarely make front-page news or television movies, and it is unlikely that anyone can recall the names of the victims. Yet, when the perpetrator is female, the consequences are very different. Our fascination with women and violence, particularly with women as perpetrators of violence, has nearly become an obsession. Yet men have murdered and mutilated women for centuries with a certain degree of tolerance, depending on particular cultural norms. For instance, in South America crimes of passion (such as husbands murdering unfaithful wives) receive only minimal attention and consequence. The reverse scenario, however, is viewed as a heinous crime, usually punished by a maximum sentence.

Amy Fisher (better known as the Long Island Lolita) received a prison term of five to fifteen years for *attempting* to murder Mary Jo Buttafuco, her married lover's wife. The story resulted in a media frenzy that continued for over a year and even spawned three separate television movies. Fisher's sentence is certainly far more severe than the eighteen months, with possible work release, that Peacock received in 1994 for the murder of his wife.

A nearly mirror image of the Amy Fisher incident involves Pamela Smart, whose teenage lover was accused of killing her husband. Who can even recall the name of her (male) teenage lover? He certainly did not receive the same media attention that Fisher did, and she did not kill anyone but perpetrated a potentially deadly assault. Fisher was portrayed as a seductive Lolita, with very little blame focused on Joey Buttafuco until later. On the other hand, in the reverse Smart scenario, the older woman was depicted as a villainous, predatory female who led her teenage lover astray. She was portrayed as the real criminal. In neither example were the men involved portrayed as being equally responsible for the crime. This uneven-handed view of female perpetrators of violence is dangerous. Given enough hype and continued repetition, almost anything can appear to have credibility, and, unfortunately, both women and men are equally likely to buy into these distorted perceptions.

The power of media myths in portraying women adds to these distorted perceptions. The portrayal of Alex, as the scorned homicidal woman in *Fatal Attraction,* is another example, with the subsequent media fallout promoting monogamy as a way of avoiding fatal-attraction relationships. In reality, all one has to do is look at domestic violence statistics to recognize the absurdity of the myth because by far most rejected stalkers and assailants are male.

Susan Smith made national headlines as a female perpetrator who killed her two children. Many people, male and female, called for her execution. Yet men have killed, brutalized, and raped their children with barely a headline. For instance, I, by chance, heard the tail end of a 1994 TV news broadcast describing how a father had explained that his four-year-old child had accidentally fallen on his hunting knife and he then killed her to end her suffering. I have been unable to find any subsequent newspaper reports about that incident.

The way in which the media report domestic violence cases also reflects the different way in which female perpetrators are depicted. Take, for example, three cases of domestic violence in Long Island, New York, reported in *Newsday* between 1995 and 1996. Two involved a husband shooting his wife and one a wife shooting her husband. The two reports of husbands as perpetrators had the following headlines: "'Say Hi to God'—Making Good on Threats, Man Shoots Wife, Self to Death" (Winslow, 1996b) and "His Deadly Rage—Man Kills Wife Who Sought Protection, Hangs Himself" (Winslow, 1996b). The third report was headlined "Cops: Woman Blasted Spouse with Shotgun, Husband Listed as Critical after Shooting" (Nash, 1995). In the first two instances the headlines include a "reason" for the murder (e.g., rage, making good on a threat) that explains the shooting or killing. In the reverse case, no reasons are given. The wife did not merely shoot or kill but "blasted spouse with shotgun," the emphasis stressing the nature of the crime, not the reason. Perhaps most revealing of the slant of the reverse scenario is the description of the woman in the third paragraph of the story: "the woman, who police said is disabled and uses a walker, was also taken to the hospital . . . where she was treated and released. It was not clear if she was injured by her husband or what her injuries were."

The image conjured up by the headline of a woman "blasting" her spouse is much different from her physical description. The most revealing aspect of the bias in reporting is the fact that the "reasons" for the male perpetrators' actions were stated in the headline, yet the possible reason (self-defense) for the woman's action is implied only several paragraphs down (allegedly even an appropriate reason): "it was not clear what her injuries were." It appears this aspect did not warrant further investigation for the story. Obviously, stereotypical biases are pervasive in the media, which lead to the perpetuation of society's expected submissive role of women in our culture.

RESEARCH FINDINGS: MEDIA, WOMEN, AND VIOLENCE

Many studies have been done on the relationship between the media and violence and on the impact that such media depictions of violence have on children. This subject will be addressed later in the chapter. There is, however, a dearth of studies on media reports and the way they portray stories of women and violence. The portrayal of women and violence by the media directly relates to the cultural acceptance of violence against women and the many societal myths concerning domestic violence. A few studies (Lemert, 1989; Schwengels & Lemert, 1986) have examined newspaper rape coverage and concluded that rape stories have fewer details than stories about murder or assault and routinely do not provide information that puts the crime into perspective.

A study analyzing the content of TV stories (Meyers, 1994a) found that female victims of violence were depicted as either totally innocent or somehow responsible for the attack, perpetuating the "virgin/whore" or "good girl/bad girl" cultural stereotypes. Perceived innocent female victims included children, the elderly, those assaulted by a mentally ill person, or those attacked by a group. When the female victim, however, was not considered helpless because of her age or disability, she was frequently represented as in some way responsible for the assault—for example, "being somewhere she should not have been," "taking a stupid risk," or "neglecting to ensure her own safety."

In an attempt to explain the "why" of violence against women, TV news reports tend to look for "reasons" that can place the blame on either the victim or the assailant. According to Pagelow (1981), "there is an interest in looking for the reasons a woman was beaten that is similar to asking why a woman was raped, unlike in other crimes . . . for example few people ask why a person was robbed."

According to Meyers (1994a), this one-sided portrayal is tied to an ideology that reflects cultural myths and patriarchal assumptions about the proper role and behavior of women. Asking why implies that it was something she said or did or perhaps wore that caused her to be beaten, raped, or killed. Portraying the victim as someone contributing to the crime further victimizes her, causing additional emotional stress. It is not unusual for victims of rape to feel guilty for having been raped. The media's reinforcement of such myths perpetuates the victim's self-blame and society's blame-the-victim perspective. Therefore, it is not surprising that the very same myths perpetuate the reasons for domestic violence—that battered women bring it upon themselves (refer to Chapter 3 for a detailed description of these myths and abusive relationships). Moreover, by presenting stories of violence against women as separate discrete events, the news media reinforce the idea that the violence was an isolated pathology or deviance. Maintaining this mirage of individual pathology, the news media deny the social roots of violence against women and absolve the larger society of any obligation to end it (Meyers, 1994a).

A study (Meyers, 1997) of news coverage of violence against women revealed that "the journalistic conception of unusualness, together with a lack of a concrete definition of news, protects reporters from charges of gender, race, and class bias, while at the same time obscures coverage that is biased against women, people of color, the poor, and the 'working class.'" The study also concluded that the reporters' reliance on police spokespersons as legitimate sources ensures that the police perspective is the predominant viewpoint represented.

Meyers interviewed nine journalists who covered crime in Atlanta to assess what they considered newsworthy. To take one example, he found that in the case of rape it would have to be unusual in that it would be particularly brutal, be part of a pattern (i.e., serial rape), involve a victim who is very young or old, or involve another criminal aspect (i.e., kidnapping or robbery). The reason given was that so many rapes are committed that it would be impossible to cover them all, and such criteria were necessary to cull out the "newsworthy" events.

It is no wonder, then, that many people believe the stereotype of the rapist lurking in the bushes. Statistics, however, show that 80 percent of women are raped by men they know, usually family, friends, or acquaintances. Consequently, news that reports only the unusual in fact reinforces the myths and the public's perception of the rapist as a deviant criminal rather than portraying rape as a pervasive social problem affecting people who are otherwise quite normal, people just like the people we are likely to know.

Soothill and Walby (1991) found in their study of newspaper coverage of sex crimes that the media "are very loath to consider that sex crimes may be related to men's and women's position in society," preferring instead to focus on a few individuals who commit atrocities (Meyers, 1994a). When the perpetrator is female, however, the reverse is true. Lorena Bobbit severed her husband's penis after he allegedly raped her. The violation was not only sensationalized, making international headlines, but resulted in frequent comments and jokes on talk shows among males as to this possibly becoming a worrisome social trend, in which other women might resort to this kind of "sadistic" violence. It cannot be emphasized too strongly in this light that 95 percent of domestic violence victims are female (U.S. Department of Justice, 1994a).

Moreover, the epidemic of violence against women has not been viewed as a major social problem until recently. Congress passed the Violent Crime Control and Law Enforcement Act of 1994, which includes the Violence Against Women Act (VAWA) of 1994. This was a landmark law because for the first time in history federal law stated that domestic violence was a crime. The act also provides grant money for various studies and the creation of a national domestic violence hot line, which was implemented in February 1996. In addition, the Clinton administration created an Office on Violence Against Women within the U.S. Department of Justice (Schornstein, 1997). This is a first step toward changing community views about domestic violence, but ingrained attitudes change very slowly. One positive aspect of the media spotlight that focused on domestic violence during the O. J. Simpson trial was that it highlighted not only the problem of domestic violence but also the many stereotypes and misconceptions surrounding the problem.

Even Pope John Paul II issued a statement (Pullella, 1996) urging women to protest media exploitation of themselves as objects of men's pleasure and power. The pope indicated that the media often undervalued or even ridiculed the role of wife and mother and depicted women in the professions as a "masculine caricature." He supported equal pay for equal work, protection for working mothers, fairness in career advancement, and equality of spouses. With regard to family rights, he said that there still was an "urgent need to achieve equality in every area." He further stated that "the advancement of women's genuine emancipation is a matter of justice, which can no longer be overlooked" and "is also a question of society's welfare." Yet, ironically, the pope also reaffirmed his unbending position against women priests in the church, saying it was justified by the Gospel. Even today, patriarchal beliefs about the role of women are deeply ingrained in religious history. The impact of these stereotypical messages appears to validate and further reinforce public opinion, policy, and even the judicial system.

MEDIA VIOLENCE AS "ENTERTAINMENT"

Violence as entertainment is evident in everyday media ranging from film, TV, radio, print, music videos, and theater, as on the New York stage in Paul Simon's musical "The Capeman." This $11 million production is about a notorious teenage killer who fatally stabbed two Hell's Kitchen youths in 1959. The highly publicized murders resulted in years of media attention with the press branding the killer, Salvador Agron, age eighteen, as "The Capeman." Agron's death sentence was later commuted, and he was released from prison in 1979. Seven years later he died of natural causes.

According to a news report (Avasthi, 1997) the play, which previewed at the end of 1997 and opened the beginning of 1998 sparked considerable controversy, with threats of boycotts and lawsuits. Parents of Murdered Children, a victim's family group, and Murder Is Not Entertainment, a watchdog group, protested the show. The controversy ignited articles as well as a cartoon captioned "It all started with 'Capeman'" appearing in the *Daily News* (November 13, 1997, see Figure 8.1). Battered by angry protests, scathing reviews, as well as production problems, the show closed several months later. However, plans were under way to develop national and international touring productions and a possible concert tour featuring the show's music (Avasthi, Morehouse, & Connor, 1998).

Many children and adolescents watch music videos. A study of music videos (Roland, 1994) found that both males and females who were rated higher in their acceptance of rape myths and stereotypes were more likely to attribute more responsibility to the women for forced sex. Obviously, the media continue to perpetuate these rape myths, which in turn serve to perpetuate acceptance of rape. In certain situations, they may actually be fu-

FIGURE 8.1

" IT ALL STARTED WITH ' CAPEMAN'... "

eling the wave of violence against women. Note also that there is serious concern not only about the content of the media's portrayal of violence but also about the increased airtime it receives. According to a recent study by the Center for Media and Public Affairs in Washington, D.C., the amount of network TV news airtime devoted to covering violent crime doubled in 1997, while the overall crime rate remained stable in the United States (Chira, 1994).

The prevalence of video games depicting repetitious murder and graphic massacre as goals of the game has also been cited as fueling the desensitization of our youth to violence. In a story about the Jonesboro, Arkansas, shooting, perpetrated by two boys ages eleven and thirteen, at a middle school resulting in the death of five and wounding of ten, the writer, Jim Dwyer (1998), makes reference to a magazine review of the new video game "Postal":

Armed with shotguns, flame-throwers and napalm, you mow down entertainingly innocent bystanders, ranging from church congregations to high school marching bands. Your maimed and dying victims beg for mercy or run around on fire, screaming for help, every so often a woman shrieks, "He's going postal."

The callous disregard for pain and suffering and the trivialization of human life and suffering were not the basis of popular games in the past. Although these games are fantasy, they nonetheless may teach a lack of empathy for others. We need to begin to study the effects on those brought up with violent video games during childhood.

Depictions of violence in the media are not merely a contemporary phenomenon; although today's media violence is often more graphic than in the past, subtle messages were apparent. For example, in the classic 1950's sitcom *The Honeymooners,* it was not unusual for beloved comedian Jackie Gleason to raise his fist toward his wife, telling her, "Alice I'm going to send you to the moon," when she was stepping out of line or he was frustrated with her behavior. Although certainly delivered in a humorous nonmalicious tone, the line held a subtle though evident implication of the expected submissive role of women and spawned a legion of men who often said the phrase to their wives.

THE IMPACT OF MEDIA VIOLENCE ON CHILDREN

Naturally, much of the public has been aroused over the impact that media portrayal of violence may have on children, who may buy into the antifemale stereotypes due to the proliferation of media messages and "infotainment" (entertainment news shows).

The exposure of American children to high levels of media violence has been well documented. The 1992 study by Huston et al. found that by the end of their teenage years children have witnessed over 200,000 violent acts on television. Add to this the increasing exposure to new cable channels and the use of VCRs, and the number increases even more. One popular film alone, *Die Hard 2,* contains depictions of 264 violent deaths. Moreover, the 1993 American Psychological Association's study on media violence concluded that higher levels of viewing violence in the mass media are correlated with increased aggressive behavior and increased acceptance of aggressive attitudes and that exposure at young ages can have lifelong consequences. More than a hundred such studies over the last forty years have shown that at least some children exposed to visual depictions of dramatic violence behave more aggressively afterward toward both inanimate objects and other children. These results have been found in both boys and girls of all social classes, races, ages, and levels of intelligence (Huesmann & Moise, 1996).

Increased airtime for showing violence is especially noteworthy, as research with adults shows a powerful tendency for viewers to overestimate the probability of events in the real world as a function of seeing these events on television (Gerbner, Gross, Morgan, & Signorielli, 1994). Thus, heavy concentrations of violence in the media tend to induce anxiety and uncertainty about future events and frequently cause sleep disturbances (Cantor, 1994). Concerns from anecdotal reports about potential emotional harm induced by violent programs that depict violent events, natural disasters, and technological disasters give rise to fright, anxiety, and upset and can result in secondary traumatization.

This tendency is even greater in children (particularly between ages seven and eleven), who have only a limited understanding of the concept of probability to help them assess what they see. They have a developing recognition that such things could happen to them, but they also naturally have far less experience with the real world (Sparks, 1994). A survey of five hundred children eight to twelve years old by *USA Today* and Nickelodeon Channel (*USA Today,* May 10, 1994) concluded that almost two-thirds of children reported having been scared or upset by violence on news shows or reality-based programs.

Consider what reports of rape and violence teach young girls, ages seven to eleven, some about to enter puberty. What kinds of impressions will develop concerning male–female relationships? Research and anecdotal reports suggest that the media's portrayal of violence and women may have a significant impact on the perceptions of men, women, and children and in the long run affect the health and well-being of our society. Studies have shown that explicit depictions of sexual violence (as in R-rated films) and graphic news stories about violence against women appear to affect the attitudes of male youths about rape and violence toward women.

The 1992 report on televised violence by the APA Task Force on Television and Society, as well as other recent research into media violence, considered the implications of exposure to sexually violent materials due to increasing opportunities for such exposure through R-rated cable and/or VCR viewing. Sexual violence in the media includes explicit sexualized violence against women, including rape and images of torture, murder, and mutilation. Films that depict women as willingly being raped have been shown to increase men's beliefs that women desire rape and deserve sexual abuse. Male youths who view sexualized violence or depictions of rape on television or in film are more likely to display callousness toward female victims of violence, especially rape.

Younger viewers often lack the critical viewing skills to discount myths about women and sexual violence, and these myths may have a deleterious influence on developing attitudes toward sexuality. A male youth's first exposure to sex may be in the form of an erotic but also violent movie, such as a slasher film, not uncommon in video movies. Thus, early attitudes are formed linking sex and violence that may be carried into adulthood. We are experiencing an epidemic in youth violence and most likely will continue to see even more desensitization to sexual violence.

One of the most obvious effects of media violence is the "copycat" violence phenomenon, in which there is a direct imitation or copying of violent or antisocial behavior. While many cases of copycat teen suicides have been documented, and there has been at least some attempt to minimize media coverage in this type of case, the same has not been true with regard to sexual violence or aggression toward women. Within a week after the murder of Nicole Simpson, a young woman in New York was gang raped, slashed forty times, and murdered. Two days later, following that report, a young woman was stabbed repeatedly and pushed from a moving car by a male companion on their first date, also in New York. Other parts of the country had similar experiences. Coincidence, or a contagious effect? New York certainly has its share of violence, but usually it involves guns; now, suddenly, the weapon of choice was a knife, wielded against a woman.

The news media claim to report reality. Rare but horrifying accounts, however, have appeared in which the reality was created for the sake of the media, for instance, in the production of underground "snuff" films, porno movies which culminate in the actual murder and dismemberment of an actress. The *New York Post* (October 1, 1975) carried a story (cited in Morgan, 1994, p. 91) about a nationwide investigation into snuff films, which were usually shot in South America and circulated on the "pornography connoisseur circuit," where select clientele could afford $1,500 for a collection of eight reels. As an example of the powerful contagious and copycat effect of the media, four months after the *Post* story ran, a porno movie called *SNUFF* opened at a first-run movie theater on Broadway in New York City, advertised as the "bloodiest thing ever filmed." More recently, allegations of a snuff film's being made were reported on an August 1994 edition of the television newsmagazine *Hard Copy*.

It can be concluded, then, that viewing media violence has three basic detrimental effects:

1. Learning aggressive and violent behavior
2. Becoming desensitized to violence and suffering
3. Becoming fearful of being victimized, including developing an increased distrust of others sometimes described as the "mean world syndrome"

RECOMMENDATIONS FOR REDUCING THE IMPACT OF MEDIA VIOLENCE

If we are to deal with the intense and sensational media coverage of violence and its impact on society, we will need to educate the public with the same level of intensity.

1. **Reduce the airtime devoted to violence.** Ideally, a reduction in the amount of media coverage of violence would prove beneficial, but it is not likely to happen in the near future. In the past, recommendations have also been made to reduce violent content during peak child viewing times (i.e., between 5 P.M. and 10 P.M.). However, unless adopted by all media outlets, possibly regulations by the Federal Communications Commission, competition for ratings will prevail, and the reduction will be thwarted.

2. **Connect violence with realistic consequences.** According to the 1996 Mediascope National Television Violence Study, perpetrators go unpunished in 73 percent of all violent scenes, thus teaching that violence is an effective means of resolving conflict. Only 16 percent of all programs portrayed negative effects (psychological, financial) of violence, yet such visual depictions of pain and suffering can actually inhibit aggressive behavior in viewers. The new trend of televising trials and showing victims' impact statements is welcome and can serve as a form of empathy training by helping the viewer understand the victim's pain and suffering. Programs highlighting the reactions and feelings of family and friends of victims should also be encouraged.

3. **Produce public service announcements and programs emphasizing antiviolence themes.** Only 4 percent of violent programs emphasize antiviolence themes (Mediascope, 1996).

4. **Develop programs that present alternatives to violence as a means of conflict resolution.** Only 13 per-

cent of reality programs depicted an alternative or methods of avoidance (Mediascope, 1996).

5. **Limit access to violence.** We should investigate and develop technologies so that parents can restrict access to inappropriate programs.

6. **Study other models of communication control.** We should investigate other models of communication, such as the Dutch model, which is controlled by a complex aggregate of religious and secular groups representing all segments of society, rather than solely businesses.

7. **Encourage positive behavior.** We can work to promote media that portray positive role models, especially for children (both girls and boys), who do assimilate the viewpoints and values with which they are bombarded. Programs portraying prosocial modes of cooperation and conflict resolution appear to increase prosocial behavior in children (Comstock & Strasburger, 1990). Today's children will be the future influences and controllers of tomorrow's media.

8. **Encourage a critical approach to media.** We can and should teach children to be media-literate, able to critically evaluate the programs they view. The same can be said for a great many adults, too.

Without question violence must be addressed from a public health perspective. Changes in media portrayal of violence will require intense public education and advocacy. The same effort needs to be expended as was done for other critical health initiatives such as smoking, drugs, and AIDS prevention, in order to have an impact on the next generation and the future direction of our society.

9

JUROR STRESS

Secondary Effects of Crime and Violence in the Course of Civic Duty

ELIZABETH K. CARLL, Ph.D.

Research on violence quite properly focuses on victims and perpetrators, but, more recently, the impact of the media's widespread coverage of violence has also begun to be scrutinized. Specifically, in light of several recent trials that gained nationwide press and TV coverage, we see that more attention needs to be paid to the effects of secondary exposure and possible secondary traumatization to those who serve as jurors. In some of the more sensational cases—for example, those involving murder, rape, or child abuse—the violence perpetrated has been especially gruesome. No surprise, then, that we have in the last few years seen reports about jurors experiencing high levels of stress in the course of their service, as evidenced in the following newspaper articles on high-profile trials:

- "Juror Says Effects of Trial Still Felt" (Hamilton, 1997) described the effects of stress during and after the bombing trial of Timothy McVeigh.

- "Jurors Are in for Another Trial: Getting Their Lives Back" (Mauro, 1995) gave accounts of the intense stress of serving on the O. J. Simpson criminal trial, the longest sequestered (266 days) jury in history.
- "Health of Dismissed Juror Big Concern" (Schatzman, 1995) described the ordeal of the twenty-six-year-old flight attendant who was rushed to the hospital, due to "nervous exhaustion," just one day after having asked to be removed from the O. J. Simpson trial jury.
- "Tempers Flared, Emotions Ran High for King Jury" (Rohrlich, 1993) discussed the intense stress of serving on the Rodney King beating trial and the related speculations about how the community might react to any verdict that the jury rendered.

SECONDARY TRAUMATIZATION AND JUROR STRESS

Traumatic events can be experienced directly and indirectly. *Secondary traumatization* (or vicarious traumatization) occurs when one witnesses serious injury or death or hears the details of a particularly traumatic or violent incident. Secondary trauma can also occur when an individual identifies with the experiences and feelings of a direct victim. Jurors are subject to this very frequently, and listening, for example, to a detailed account of how a person was taken hostage or the grotesque description of a baby's body being cut up and fed to the family dog is a horrible experience. The continual repetition of gruesome details and heart-wrenching stories common in some trials forces jurors to relive the traumas and identify with victims, setting the stage for possible secondary traumatization. The symptoms typical of acute and posttraumatic stress are as follows:

- Sadness/depression
- Anger and irritability
- Poor concentration

- Forgetfulness
- Social withdrawal
- Sleep disturbances and nightmares
- Stomach distress
- Flashbacks and disturbing intrusive thoughts
- Emotional numbing—denial, compartmentalization, and isolation of the traumatic event
- Cold-/flulike symptoms—usually chronic situations
- Worsening of existing medical conditions (e.g., ulcers, migraine, etc.)
- Avoidance of stimuli associated with trauma
- Loss of feeling secure in the world
- Elevated blood pressure

It is important to keep in mind that jurors are selected at random from jury rolls. They come from all walks of life and in many instances have little or no experience with the kinds of violence they may have to deal with in the course of a trial. The effects of stress on jurors serving on these difficult cases, therefore, are similar to those experienced by disaster victims or those who have witnessed crimes, violence, and horrific accidents. Some jurors may well experience one or more of the stress-related symptoms listed here, and these symptoms may often extend past the end of the trial and leave a lasting imprint on the juror. They may interfere with the juror's return to daily life and may continue for several weeks or months or, in some instances, even longer.

THE TRANSITION FROM ACUTE STRESS TO POSTTRAUMATIC STRESS DISORDER

A diagnosis of *acute stress disorder* is made when symptoms occur during or immediately after an event or trauma, last for at least two days, and may continue for four weeks after the conclusion of the traumatic event. When symptoms persist beyond one month, a diagnosis of posttraumatic stress disorder may be appropriate (American Psychiatric Association, 1994). The severity, proximity, and duration of an individual's exposure to a traumatic event are the most important factors in determining the likelihood of developing stress reactions. Lengthy and difficult trials, therefore, make it likely that at least some jurors will develop stress reactions and disorders. It is also important to emphasize that posttraumatic stress reactions are normal reactions by normal people reacting to abnormal events and do not presume preexisting stress, which indeed may be present in certain jurors.

COMPONENTS OF A STRESSFUL TRIAL

Because the impression a community has of juror service helps determine its willingness to serve, the need to understand the effects of stressful trials takes on significant civic importance. There are some recent examinations of this problem (Hafemeister, 1993; Hafemeister & Ventis, 1996; Hafemeister & Ventis, 1992; Kaplan & Winget, 1992; Kelley, 1994; Shuman, Hamilton, & Daley, 1994). As media coverage of sensational trials shows no sign of diminishing, we need to look at what particular factors make a trial especially stressful and what effect these stresses have on the citizens who serve as jurors.

Cases Involving Violence and Gruesome Evidence

Repeated exposure to photos, videos, and reenactments of extreme violence and brutality can have a telling effect on jurors, and cases involving children as victims may be especially traumatic. The photos of rescue personnel carrying the debris-covered bodies of children from the rubble after the Murrah Building bombing in Oklahoma City or the horrific autopsy photos of Nicole Brown Simpson and Ron Goldman during the O. J. Simpson trial could not help but leave vivid impressions in jurors' memories. Continual repetition of sometimes gruesome details in such cases forces the jurors to relive the events over and over again. Technological strategies to enhance the impact of evidence (blowups, computer simulations, etc.) also make the experience even more disturbing.

Not all trials of heinous crimes, however, receive wide media attention. Take, for example, the 1992 trial of Jason Radtke, perhaps the most gruesome trial in New York state history, which received only minimal coverage. Radtke was convicted of killing his six-day-old son in a fit of rage because the infant urinated on him. He then chopped up the baby and fed it to the family German shepherd, to hide the evidence. The child's mother reported that she feigned sleep in another room for fear of her life and that of her young daughter. Part of the intensely emotional and horrific testimony was reported in *New York Newsday* (Taylor, 1992):

> Her voice quavering and tears streaming down her face, Linda Boyce, 21, described how she was awakened August 10, 1990, by the sounds of the German shepherd eating. "I woke up and the dog was eating something," Boyce said. "I heard crunching and I heard Jason (Radtke, her boyfriend) breathing like he was upset," Boyce said. "He had his back in my direction and there was blood all over the floor . . . he had blood on his arms." Boyce told how Radtke commanded the dog to eat. The dog "had the skin . . . flesh in his mouth," Boyce said.

The trial was especially gruesome as autopsy photos of the dog's stomach and baby's remains were examined to determine whether the baby's injuries had jagged or straight edges. This measure was necessary to rule out the possibility of the dog having attacked and bit the child. Three members of the jury ran out of the courtroom and vomited as the evidence was being presented. The night before the verdict was rendered, three jurors were taken to the hospital to be treated for stress-related problems. Justice David Goldstein, the presiding judge, recognized the stress the jurors were experiencing and arranged to have immediate counseling (critical incident stress debriefing) available at the trial's conclusion.

As a trauma expert and founder and coordinator of the New York State Psychological Association's volunteer Disaster/Crisis Response Network, I was called in to debrief the jury. During the course of the debriefing (and the follow-up sessions that were requested by some of the jurors), the jurors reported that they were experiencing sleeping and eating problems, nightmares, intrusive repetitive thoughts about the details of the case, anxiety, depression, flashbacks, difficulty in concentrating, headaches, heart palpitations, and elevated blood pressure. In fact, one of the jurors reported an elevation in blood pressure requiring a brief hospitalization, increase in blood pressure medication, and physician recommendation to take some time off before going back to work.

Feedback from the jurors and the trial judge indicated that the debriefing and follow-up counseling were extremely helpful in ameliorating the effects of the stress and assisting the jurors with the readjustment to their daily lives. The jurors were very appreciative of the help they received and the concern expressed by Justice Goldstein (and the criminal justice system) for their welfare.

With growing awareness of the need to address jury stress, the Unified Court System of New York State has included training (Carll, 1995a) for judges as part of their annual training seminars. Unfortunately, to date no court systems have established a program for psychological debriefing of jurors after very stressful trials. Even with studies documenting the effects of stress, such as that of Shuman et al. (1994) that found that jurors serving on traumatic trials were six times more likely to show symptoms associated with depression, change takes place very slowly. At present the availability of such counseling service for jurors depends on individual judges' awareness and discretion.

Serving on Highly Publicized and/or Controversial Cases

The *National Law Journal* conducted a survey of fifty jurors who served on high-profile cases since 1992, including the Rodney King, William Kennedy Smith, and Jim Bakker trials. It found that 62 percent of the jurors stated that they experienced stress from jury service, whereas 38 percent did not or did not know whether they had. Other reports of the possible negative effects of stress were also increasingly reported in the news. According to one news report (Gannett News Service, June 23, 1992), a jury foreman suffered a fatal heart attack in the course of a widely publicized New York state case, and his wife blamed it on stress associated with serving as foreman.

Highly publicized cases rendering unpopular verdicts can be especially stressful. In the Rodney King trial, a juror was quoted as saying "jurors suffered all kinds of physical and psychological repercussions after the not guilty verdict" (Malnic, 1993). The subsequent Los Angeles riots serve as a vivid reminder to future jurors of the possible consequences (e.g., harassment, threats) that may result from controversial verdicts. Moreover, the glare of the media spotlight and unwelcome public attention can further exacerbate an already tense situation for the jurors when they attempt to resume their normal lives after the trial. Similar stresses were apparent in the O. J. Simpson trial, during which racial issues were brought to the forefront and concern about the possible community repercussions were discussed nightly on television by legal pundits. The jurors were caught in a vise, as it were, being compelled to deal with a public situation over which they had no control.

Sometimes juries can be presented with untenable options because of legal decisions made by the prosecution or the defense, or both. The 1997 trial of Louise Woodward, a nineteen-year-old English au pair who was charged with the death of an eight-month-old child she was caring for, is a startling example. Woodward was accused of shaking the infant so violently in a fit of temper that he died. The prosecution charged her with murder, and her defense counsel adopted the strategy of asking that the jury be given only the choice of convicting her of murder, rather than the perhaps more appropriate choice of manslaughter, or acquitting her completely. The jury, after deliberating for twenty-seven hours, found her guilty of murder in the second degree, which carries a sentence of life imprisonment. That decision caused an outcry in England and the United States as being far too harsh for the circumstances.

In a striking turnaround, the trial judge, Hiller B. Zobel, reduced the charge from murder to involuntary manslaughter and sentenced Woodward to just the time she had already served in jail. Most public opinion seemed to feel that it was a mistake for the defense to insist that the choice be only between a very severe sentence or acquittal. In his decision, Judge Zobel said, "I believe that the circumstances in which the Defendant acted were characterized by confusion, inexperience, frustration, immaturity, and some anger, but not malice (in the legal sense) supporting a conviction of second-degree murder" (Goldberg, 1997). One juror, on hearing that the judge's decision would obviate the need for a new trial, said that this knowledge "is a great relief to me personally."

In another news report (Kennedy, November 11, 1997), a juror said that he would like to ask the judge why he changed the verdict from murder to manslaughter, after telling the jurors that they could not consider the lesser charge. "Why were we boxed into having three lousy choices?" asked the juror. Several other jurors stated that although a life sentence was excessive, Woodward should serve some jail time. A juror also indicated that some of his fellow jurors have received angry phone calls from strangers. "I'm surprised there was so much animosity toward the jury," he said.

Clearly jurors can be put in an extremely stressful situation by the legal maneuverings of prosecution and defense. Jurors are there to make decisions. If the only choices available to them, however, seem inappropriate, the decision-making process can become incredibly painful.

Trials with Sharply Divided Opinions, Acrimonious Debate, or a Lone Dissent

The report (Libertarian Party of Colorado, 1996) of the trial of a nineteen-year-old woman charged with felony possession of a controlled substance that ended in a mistrial is yet another example of stressful jury duty. The lone dissenting juror, Laura Kriho, reported that several of the jurors began verbally attacking her and ridiculing her reasonable doubt. One juror sent a note to the judge alleging that Kriho improperly told other jurors what sentences the defendant might face if convicted. As a result, the judge declared a mistrial, and Kriho herself was tried in October 1996 and convicted in February 1997 (and subsequently fined $1,200) for contempt of court for failing to volunteer information to the court during jury selection. Her attorney has filed an appeal to overturn the conviction (Smith, 1997). Paul Grant, Kriho's attorney, stated that the conviction should give every potential juror in the state pause:

> It's now been determined that jurors have a legal duty to confess to any prior sins in their life and to their political beliefs, so that the court can decide whether or not it wants them on the jury. Even though the juror hasn't been asked these questions, this case suggests they now have a legal duty to provide that information, even if they are not asked, and it's criminal if they don't.

According to Grant, "in convicting Kriho and by creating a new law, jurors who think independently, or who have skeletons in the closet can be targeted for their beliefs and lifestyles" (Hauser, 1997). What is of interest in this case is that it appears to be the first of its kind, an instance in which a juror who held a lone dissenting opinion appears to have been punished for her beliefs/behavior.

Examples of acrimonious deliberations and divided opinions have also been the subject of films. The 1957 film *Twelve Angry Men* depicted the inner workings of jury deliberations. The intense deliberations forced the jurors to examine their own assumptions about life, and for one of the jurors it became a shattering experience. The 1996 film *The Juror* highlighted the potential perils of jury duty and the intense process of deliberations.

Trials Raising Concern for Personal Safety or Possible Retaliation

Trials involving organized crime or gangs can be stressful if jurors fear intimidation and retaliation after the verdict. Fear of gang violence upon returning to the same community in which a defendant, who is a gang member, resides may be very intimidating.

Stress Due to Lengthy Trials and Sequestration

Separation from one's family and friends for an extended period removes the normal social supports on which we all rely. Extended absences can result in significant changes in a relationship. One's boy- or girlfriend may strike up another relationship. Returning to a household in which a spouse has had to make independent daily decisions may present quite a different situation from the one existing before the separation. Questions of decision making and control may become sources of conflict.

Prolonged sequestration itself can cause stress. Some have likened it to living under conditions similar to those for a prisoner of war, in which one is locked up and mail, newspapers, and television are censored. Lack of privacy for phone calls and long confinement with strangers with whom they may have nothing in common all contribute to jurors' flaring tempers and stress. The longest sequestered jury in history (266 days, for the O. J. Simpson trial) had six jurors removed for misconduct. Four months into the trial, the jury defied Judge Lance Ito and refused to hear the case until a grievance concerning several deputies supervising the sequestration was resolved. Stress from sequestration also became apparent in the Reginald Denny case, in which one juror reportedly was running down the halls of the hotel, shouting, "I can't take it anymore" (*Washington Post,* 1993).

Sequestration may also have an impact on jury decision making. It can push jurors to retaliate against a defendant or to abandon their own deeply held feelings and go along with other jurors' decisions just to get out (DeAngelis, 1995). In fact, because of reports of the tension that sequestration creates, the New York state court system revoked a long-standing rule that juries in all criminal trials had to be sequestered during deliberations (Roan, 1995).

The Nature of the Jury Process Itself Contributing to the Stress

Jurors recognize the enormous responsibility and gravity of rendering verdicts, especially in decisions involving capital punishment or possible life imprisonment. The stress of carrying out this responsibility can certainly take its toll. In recent years, many states have reinstituted the death penalty, and more seem inclined to do so. Not infrequently, the media and those in public office have encouraged the prosecution in certain trials to ask for the death penalty. Such public pressure, however, has shown little concern for the jurors who are the ones who will have to vote for conviction and then handle the stress of making such a decision.

It is important to remember here that emergency and rescue personnel receive advance training to be able to perform their jobs and deal with the accompanying stress. They also have had the option of choosing their line of work. Obviously such points do not apply to the average citizen who finds him- or herself selected to serve on a stressful trial or face making a life-and-death decision—situations for which the juror may be entirely unprepared.

Finally, it should also be noted that the opportunity to seek support from others and discuss one's feelings is not available to jurors, as they are not permitted to discuss the case with others out of court. Being able to discuss one's feelings with others is a basic component of stress reduction; being bereft of that option makes the juror's situation just that more stressful.

INTERVENTION AND STRESS MANAGEMENT STRATEGIES

Because a summons to jury duty is unanticipated, it can always be a cause of some anxiety for most jurors, even well before they begin hearing any distressing testimony or viewing grisly evidence. They must immediately begin to make plans for taking care of their work and family obligations. One of my patients described it this way: "I had to do extra loads of wash, prepare meals ahead of time so I could freeze them because I wouldn't have time to shop, arrange for rides for my daughter's piano and dance lessons and afternoon tutoring, and write up lesson plans for the sub who will be teaching my class." Others, of course, have to take time to arrange their work affairs so that colleagues can handle whatever comes up in their absence. So jury duty begins by disrupting people's daily lives, making some of them even more vulnerable to the anxieties fostered by a difficult or long drawn-out case. When jurors prepare for their absence during the term of service, they will have taken a great step toward reducing stress.

Strategies for Jurors to Manage Stress

Both jurors and judges can and should take steps to lessen the stress of jury duty. Following are some suggestions for jurors:

- **Prepare.** Organizing and delegating workloads so as not to be faced with a mountain of work and disorganization upon returning home can go a long way to putting one's mind at ease. Usually a juror has about two weeks between receipt of the summons and the beginning of service. Use this time to enlist the support of family, friends, and coworkers. Make sure that everyone realizes that normal routines will be disrupted and that all will have to pitch in to take up the slack. The most difficult part of the planning is the uncertainty of the term of service. A juror may not be selected for a trial and be finished in a matter of days. On the other hand, the term of service may be prolonged, so flexibility is crucial for any plan.

- **Keep a journal.** While on jury duty, many jurors find it helpful to jot down brief notes day by day. This can be very helpful in venting and releasing thoughts and feelings. Having such an outlet can become important because discussion of the trial among jurors is not permitted, except during the final deliberations. Journal writing can be especially useful in cases in which the juror feels inhibited about verbally expressing certain thoughts and feelings.

- **Keep occupied.** Bring in your favorite audiotapes, CDs, or a book. Some jurors bring work with them that can be done out of the office. This approach is especially helpful when sequestered jurors are not permitted to discuss the case. Being able to distract oneself from unpleasant details and proceedings facilitates relaxation and reduces stress. Being able to accomplish some work chores also lessens anxiety about job responsibilities and guilt about putting extra pressure on coworkers.

- **Acknowledge group decision making.** Deciding another person's future—in some instances even whether he or she lives or dies—places an enormous burden on an individual. Recognizing that the final decision is not made by any one individual but rests with the group will serve to minimize possible self-imposed guilt or second-guessing after the trial. Jury duty does impose a sometimes harsh task on individuals, but they must see that they are not just individuals but part of a system. Maybe it is not an ideal system, but it is the only one we have.

- **Use the group as a source of support during the trial.** Exchanging life experiences and even striking up friendships can provide an opportunity for social support separate from the trial issues.

- **Use the group for support after the trial.** It is not unusual to have close bonds form among jurors during the course of stressful trials. For example, during the course of debriefing after the Radtke murder trial, the jurors decided to meet the following week at a neighborhood restaurant. The group also met several times over the course of the next few months. Getting together provided an outlet for discussing mutual concerns and experiences at a time when friends and family may no longer be interested in hearing about the trial.

- **Do not take things personally.** For some individuals, jury duty may be their first group experience in dealing with sometimes sharply divided opinions that have to be resolved eventually into some kind of consensus. A juror may feel overwhelmed, intimidated, even attacked by others who do not agree with his or her point of view. Although it may be helpful, it is unlikely that in the near future jurors will receive a brief course in group dynamics and conflict resolution. Therefore, frequently reminding oneself during heated debates that the focus must remain on the defendant will help objectify the arguments. It is not the juror who is on trial, after all.

Strategies for Judges to Help Manage Juror Stress

Judges can play an important role here, and their awareness of the problems jurors may be facing can help prevent unfortunate incidents that may force a retrial. Following are some suggestions to judges on how to help jurors deal with their stresses.

- **Be sensitive to stress-related symptoms.** Knowing what signs to look for helps judges focus on and be more aware of jurors' reactions during the course of a trial. Typical signs of juror stress include crying, frequently looking away from evidence, tuning out, and looking as if not there. Being responsive to these signs is important, as overwhelmed and stressed individuals no longer process information effectively. Scheduling the morning and afternoon breaks with this in mind will be helpful to the jury, giving them a break after hearing anxiety-provoking testimony.

- **Monitor the flow of evidence when possible.** Repeated exposure to depictions of photos, videos, and reenactments of extreme violence and brutality have a powerful negative effect on jurors. Cases involving children as victims may be especially traumatic. Continual repetition of sometimes gruesome and unpleasant de-tails forces jurors to relive the events over and over again, and, whenever possible, judges should try to limit the continual repetition of gruesome evidence and grisly details.

- **Offer counseling after the trial.** Recommendations by a trial judge for immediate counseling following a stressful trial would be most welcome. Such suggestions are especially beneficial in that they alert the jury to the need for this kind of specialized help to reduce stress. They also serve to destigmatize preconceived notions about psychological counseling, presenting it as a service that is helpful for all in the line of civic duty.

General Suggestions for the Judicial System for Managing Juror Stress

A judge who observes stress can arrange for follow-up specialized counseling, usually referred to as critical incident debriefing or, as I prefer to describe it, *critical incident stress intervention* (CISI). The term *debriefing* is somewhat misleading because the proceeding is not a fact-finding session or discussion; rather, it focuses on ventilating the emotions and other negative reactions called up by the incident. A *critical incident* is defined as any event that has the capability of overwhelming a person's usual coping ability.

Usually such CISI sessions are conducted in groups in which individuals can gain awareness, information, and stress management strategies. A session may take an average of two to three hours and should ideally be conducted within twenty-four to seventy-two hours following the incident. One key element in these sessions is the opportunity they provide for trauma victims to hear others verbalize thoughts and feelings that they themselves might hesitate to raise for fear of being perceived as abnormal or weak. Just knowing that one's fears and stresses are shared by others can have a very powerful effect in accelerating the recovery process. Mental health professionals with specialized training should conduct the group and individual CISIs, as it is imperative to assess what issues to address during the course of the CISI and what issues should not be broached, in order to provide the most effective and useful stress reduction intervention.

Courts in several states have provided single-session counseling programs or debriefings to jurors in certain cases, such as high-profile murder trials that included gruesome and graphic evidence and testimony. These interventions and debriefing sessions are similar to those used to help victims and relief workers involved in disasters and other traumatic events, especially violent crimes. It is also important to suggest that a similar stress intervention program be made available for court personnel, who may be repeatedly involved in stressful and traumatic trials and handle gruesome evidence again and again.

From a societal perspective, many individuals' only contact with the judicial system comes as a result of jury duty. It would be most unfortunate if the experience should adversely affect their well-being and increase the likelihood of their attempting to avoid further participation in the system. It would clearly be beneficial—for the citizens who serve as jurors, for the community, and for the judicial system as a whole—to have in place programs designed to minimize the adverse effects of stress and possible secondary traumatization related to serving on a jury. Such stress intervention programs can demonstrate that the judicial system is aware and appreciative of the contributions of citizens while carrying out their civic responsibilities and that the judicial system is concerned about improving the quality of life of all members of the community.

10

CONCLUSION

ELIZABETH K. CARLL, Ph.D.

On December 2, 1997, the *New York Times* carried a story of a fourteen-year-old boy in West Paducah, Kentucky, who "drew a gun . . . and shot eight students who had just finished a prayer meeting in a high school lobby here." Three girls died in the shooting. Terrible as this story is, perhaps the most chilling and revealing aspect of the incident was the young gunman's reaction afterward. "I'm sorry," he said to Bill Bond, the principal of the school. Bond reported, "He acted just like he had been caught with some minor offense."

If there is one point that has come up again and again during the course of this book, it is the deeply troubling sense of disconnection on the part of so many perpetrators of violence from the consequences of their violent acts. It is not even that they lack remorse for what they did. It is that in so many cases, as the one cited here, they seem almost totally oblivious to the loss, grief, and pain they have inflicted. The perpetrators often seem simply not to perceive others as really existing, with lives, loves, and hopes of their own. They seem to think that others exist merely for their own use and can be cavalierly abused or beaten or even worse. A terrible loss of empathy runs throughout all segments of our society.

The danger of such extreme alienation—and the toll it exacts at work, at home, and in the community—is demonstrated throughout this book, which has used both research and numerous examples of real-life events. The purpose of the book has not been to catalogue a theoretical compendium of violence; enough of that is already on the market. Rather, the intention has been to make available to the reader the latest, cutting-edge information and research on violence to help understand the many interrelated facets of violence and formulate effective interventions and, ultimately, to help minimize this devastating social problem. Personal safety is not a benign gift of the state but an inherent right that all citizens, including children, should enjoy. It is the very hallmark of a civilized society, and its lack must not be tolerated.

WE ARE NOT HELPLESS

A major focal point of this book is that we are not helpless in the face of violence. There are steps we all can take to reduce the chance of it happening and to recover from the psychological effects of violent events when they do happen.

In the Workplace

The study of violence in the workplace was discussed first in this book, because it is a venue where all the interrelated aspects of violence in our society meet. Violence in the workplace can involve interpersonal violence (as when a coworker explodes and attacks those around him), family violence (as when a employee is attacked at her workplace by a spouse or boyfriend), and community violence (as in a terrorist attack or hostage-taking situation.) Although such events cannot be prevented across the board, a number of signs and clues have been elucidated in order that management and security people of a company or government office may be able to detect the possibility of a violent event and perhaps head it off. In addition, the importance of professional preplanning by management for dealing with the fallout from a violent event has been discussed. Such planning is crucial because not only does it aid employees to recover from trauma and shock but it also gives them a sense that the company cares. This reestablishment of a sense of community is most critical in those incidents involving impersonal and random violence (e.g., a terrorist bombing). A caring community is the best defense against the disorientation caused by such events.

Other aspects of violence that impinge on the workplace have also been covered, such as stalking and crisis and hostage negotiations—all with an eye toward providing information and effective interventions that can help prevent or minimize the damage from such incidents. Implementing the recommendations in these cases will go a long way toward controlling them and helping victims recover from the effects of trauma. The recommendations are sound, based on the latest research, and they can prove invaluable to everyone in management, police work, emergency health services, mental health services, and the public in general.

In the Home

Unfortunately, the home is frequently the most dangerous place to be, especially for women. The problem of violence toward women and children has been emphasized because it is by far the most common form of domestic violence. Marital discord, family problems, and personal relationships cause stress for everyone—stress that can (and very often does) erupt into violent behavior, as the extraordinary incidence of battered women and abused children so clearly shows.

In this area, in addition to having made practical recommendations for dealing with intolerable situations, the book has outlined the need to change the way we perceive women and men. We simply must rethink the way men, women, and society view the role of women and children in the home. The myths commonly accepted about rape and abuse in the family have been discussed in detail. We must get past the idea that a man's wife and children are his chattels, to be done with as he thinks fit. We must work to educate the public, especially young boys and girls, that force and violence are *not*—are *never*—the answers to a stressful situation. A punch in the mouth, a kick, the threat of something much worse are not problem solvers.

We must also educate the legal system, the police, the health and social service system, and the media to stop trivializing family abuse. "She provoked me" is not an explanation or an excuse, and police, law, and the media must stop taking it for one. If this book can help change the way our society views the use of force on women and children, I will consider it a great success.

The special problems arising from disputes about child custody and visitation rights have also been addressed, including violent parent(s). The kinds of interventions provided by law, and how they may be implemented and how, in certain cases, they may work to make matters even worse, are important to understand. Weighing alternatives in such cases is crucial. Considerable detail has been cited to explain the pros and cons of different approaches in specific instances.

It is imperative that violent behavior, even if directed at a spouse, must be considered during custody and visitation hearings. Take, for example, the recent report (Associated Press, December 3, 1997) of a thirty-five-year-old Tennessee man, Darryl Keith Holton, who shot and killed his three sons, ages seven, ten, and thirteen, and a four-year-old girl his former wife had had with another man, because he was afraid he would never gain custody of them. According to the news report, "Crystal Holton allowed the children to visit her former husband so they could go Christmas shopping. She said she had kept the children away from him for 2 1/2 months after filing an Order of Protection because 'he beat the crap out of me.' She said he loved the children especially her daughter." After turning himself in to the police, Holton told the detectives that he took the children to the repair shop at which he worked and told them to close their eyes and then shot them with a semiautomatic assault rifle.

Important issues concerning the problem of stalking have also been discussed. The legal procedures available to stalking victims have been examined here in detail. More important, the procedures described have been evaluated as to how they work in specific cases in order to effect the desired outcome. For instance, examples of cases have been given in which seeking and obtaining a restraining order actually worsened the situation. Also presented has been the relatively novel idea of encouraging stalking victims to change from focusing on the behavior of the stalker, to changing their own behavior in order to lessen possible contacts with the stalker. Thus, even with this very serious problem (estimates are that 90 percent of the instances in which women were killed by husbands or boyfriends involved stalking), practical and effective interventions and strategies are available. The discussion of stalking included in this book will prove invaluable to anyone caught up in such a situation.

In the Community

The vast majority of people, when asked about the safety of their neighborhoods, will rate it as acceptable or better. It is always the neighborhood "over there" that is bad and dangerous. As seen in the course of this book, the phrase "It can't happen here" is a common delusion. Violence, crime, and abuse do not recognize geographic borders or social class. In addition to addressing the previously mentioned problems concerning violence, two chapters have focused specifically on growing issues of community and public interest: media depiction of violence and juror stress.

The discussion of the way violence is depicted in the media is of major importance, as the media have an enormous impact in shaping public opinion. The focus of this discussion has not been so much the actual depiction of violent acts in the media, especially TV (although that medium is included), but more so on the culture of violence that surrounds the depictions. It is essential to change that culture because it perpetuates myths and biases, especially about women that foster perceptions that they are objects to be used rather than people to be respected.

Numerous examples have been cited in the book of print and TV news that trivializes, even ignores, violence against women.

Evidence has been cited as to how such stories are exploited for their sensational value, but the actual pain and empathy for the victim downplayed or omitted altogether. The casual acceptance of the idea that husbands and boyfriends may use force on their partners with very little reaction from the press and other institutions has been described here. Also provided have been examples of how, when they perpetrate a violent act, women are viewed by the public as extreme malefactors and receive punishment far in excess of that a man would receive for the same act. A change in this attitude is slowly evolving, but we must do much more to combat this biased view of women's proper role in our society. Most important, we need to address the insidious idea that using violence to settle problems is somehow macho and admirable—an idea, unfortunately, that is often reinforced by the media. Men can be valiant and heroic, but beating women and children is no way to show it. It is particularly important to stress this point with boys and young men. Violent children will likely grow up to be violent adults and the violence will spread throughout the community, resulting in a self-perpetuating culture of violence.

Also covered has been a relatively new topic in this area: the stress often experienced by jurors who must sit on cases involving particularly horrible crimes and capital punishment. Because jurors must serve as part of their civic responsibility, they have very little control over the cases to which they may be assigned. Some may be totally unprepared, psychologically, for the kinds of testimony they may be subjected to. Many may not be ready to make a life-or-death decision. Recommendations have been made here for the legal system to demonstrate concern for the stresses that jurors may experience in certain cases and to take steps to ameliorate the effects of these stresses. Tips have been offered for jurors on how to prepare for serving, so that they can mitigate some of the disruption that long or difficult trials may bring to their lives, as well as cope with very stressful trials. We need the jury system to make our form of legal justice work, but society must also be aware of the occasional costs that such service incurs. The citizens who serve on juries provide a vital public function, and society and the legal system must ensure that the people who perform it are not harmed by the experience.

Summing Up

In short, this book is a plea for a more humane approach than that of our culture of violence. It is a practical book, and an informed one. A culture of violence will continue to exist unless every aspect of violence is no longer tolerated, whether it is against women or children or occurs in the workplace, home, or community. Tolerance of violence at any given point will result in seepage into other areas much like a cancer that metastasizes, ultimately spreading throughout the body. What begins as a few cancer cells, left untreated, can ultimately devastate the body.

The recommendations put forth in this book are realistic and sensible suggestions. They involve nothing more than what a truly civilized society owes to itself and its citizens. They do not require that we remake the world. They ask mostly that we change our thinking and thereby change our actions. They ask primarily that we recognize the pain and grief that violence inflicts and that we forego its routine use as a medium of settling disputes. They ask, finally, that we make this message clear (through all media) to ourselves and our children, in the workplace, in the home, and in the community.

REFERENCES

Ackerman, M. J. (1995). *Clinician's guide to child custody evaluations*. New York: Wiley.

American Psychiatric Association. (1994). *Diagnostic and statistical manual of mental disorders* (4th ed.). Washington, DC: Author.

American Psychological Association. (1993). *Violence and youth: Psychology's response: Vol. 1: Summary Report of the American Psychological Association Commission on Violence and Youth*. Washington, DC: Author.

American Psychological Association Task Force on Television and Society. (1992). Report on televised violence. Washington, DC: Author.

APA Presidential Task Force on Violence and the Family. (February 21, 1996). Witnessing violence in childhood can lead to violence in adulthood, says new report. *APA News Release*.

Arizona Revised Statutes Annotated, sec 25-332(B) (Supp. 1993).

Arkow, P. (1992). The correlations between cruelty to animals and child abuse and the implications for veterinary medicine. *Canadian Veterinary Journal, 33*, 518–521.

Arkow, P. (1994). Child abuse, animal abuse and the veterinarian. *Journal of the American Veterinary Medical Association, 204*, 1004–1007.

Ascione, F. (1993). Children who are cruel to animals: A review of research and implications for developmental psychopathology. *Anthrozoos, 6*, 226–247.

Associated Press. (October 19, 1994). Furor on sentencing 1^1/$_2$-year term for killing wife. *Newsday*, p. A04.

Associated Press. (March 12, 1995). Killing a law firm. *Newsday*.

Associated Press. (July 15, 1995). Marriage ordered in Ohio abuse case. *Newsday,* p. A4.

Associated Press. (October 19, 1997). Man kills wife for infidelity; gets 18 months. *New York Times.*

Associated Press. (October 22, 1997). Young mother shot as her kids watch. *Newsday,* p. A25.

Associated Press. (December 2, 1997). Gun fire inside a school kills 3 and wounds 5. *New York Times,* p. A18.

Associated Press. (December 3, 1997). Custody dispute ends with 4 children slain. *Newsday.*

Avasthi, S. (November 9, 1997). "Capeman": Strikes a sour note. *New York Post.*

Avasthi, S., Morehouse III, W., & Connor, T. (March 6, 1998). It's curtains for top flop Capeman. *New York Post.*

Bachrnan, R., & Saltzman, L. E. (1995). Violence against women: Estimates from the redesigned survey: NCJ–154348. Washington, DC: Bureau of Justice Statistics, U.S. Department of Justice.

Barnett, O. W., Miller-Perrin, C. L., & Perrin, R. D. (1996). *Family violence across the lifespan.* Newbury Park, CA: Sage.

Beck, A. (1981). In B. Fogel (Ed.), *Interrelations between people and pets* (p. 232). Springfield, IL: C.C. Thomas, cited by Ascione 1993.

Besharov, D. J. (1990). *Recognizing child abuse.* New York: Free Press.

Big cases bring lots of stress. (February 22, 1993). *National Law Journal,* p. S14.

Blackwood, R. E. (1993). The context of news photos: Roles portrayed by men and women. *Journalism Quarterly, 60,* 710–714.

Blumer, D., & Benson, D. F. (1982). Psychiatric manifestations of epilepsy. In D. F. Benson & D. Blumer (Eds.), *Psychiatric aspects of neurologic disease* (Vol. 2, pp. 25–47). New York: Grune & Stratton.

Blumer, D., & Migeon, C. (1975). Hormone and hormonal agents in the treatment of aggression. *Journal of Nervous and Mental Disorders, 160,* 27–137.

Bolton, F. G., & Bolton, S. R. (1987). *Working with violent families: A guide for clinical and legal practioners.* Newbury Park, CA: Sage.

Bond, A. J. (1992). Pharmacological manipulation of aggressiveness and impulsiveness in healthy volunteers. *Progress in Neuro-Psychopharmacology & Biological Psychiatry, 16,* 1–7.

Bond, A., & Lader, M. (1979). Benzodiazapines and aggression. In M. Sandler (Ed.), *Psychopharmacology of aggression* (pp. 173–182). New York: Raven.

Breslau, N., Davis, G. C., Andreski, P., & Peterson, E. (1991). Traumatic events and post traumatic stress disorder in an urban population of young adults. *Archives of General Psychiatry, 48,* 216–222.

Browne, A. (1987*). When battered women kill.* New York: Free Press.

Brownmiller, S. (1975). *Against our will: Men, women, and rape.* Toronto: Bantam.

Buel, S. M. (1996). *Toward a safer existence: Trends and innovative developments,* Atlanta, GA: National College of District Attorneys.

Calhoun, K. S., & Atkeson, B. M. (1991). *Treatment of rape victims: Facilitating psychosocial adjustment.* New York: Pergamon.

Campbell, M., Perry R., & Green, W. H. (1984): Use of lithium in children and adolescents. *Psychosomatics, 25,* 95–106.

Cantor, J. (1994). Fright reactions to mass media. In J. Bryand & D. Zillman (Eds.), *Media effects: Advances in theory and research* (pp. 213–245). Hillsdale, NJ: Lawrence Erlbaum.

Carll, E. K. (1991). *Dealing with anticipatory, acute, and chronic stress related to trauma situations.* Paper presented at the American Psychological Association Annual Convention, San Francisco, CA.

Carll, E. K. (1992). *Psychological trauma: Intervention and treatment strategies.* Paper presented at the New York State Psychological Association Annual Convention, Bolton Landing, NY.

Carll, E. K. (1994). Psychological perspective on the media's portrayal of women and violence. Paper presented at the American Psychological Association Annual Convention. Los Angeles, CA.

Carll, E. K. (1995a). *Juror stress: Interventions and strategies for judges.* Paper presented at the 1995 Annual Judicial Seminars, New York State Unified Court System. Tarrytown, NY.

Carll, E. K. (1995b). Trauma psychology: Psychological intervention in the aftermath of disaster and crisis. In L. VandeCreek, S. Knapp, & T. L. Jackson (Eds.), *Innovations in clinical practice: A sourcebook.* Sarasota, FL: Professional Resource Press.

Carll, E. K. (1995c). Victims of violence and the development of eating disorders. *New York State Psychologist, 7,* 28.

Center on Crime. (August 5, 1997). Communities and culture: Research tool on domestic violence available on the Internet. *M2 PressWire.*

Charlow, A. (1994). Awarding custody: The best interests of the child and other fictions. In S. Humm, B. Ort, M. Anbari, W. Lader, & W. Biel (Eds.), *Child, parent and state* (pp. 3–26). Philadelphia: Temple University Press.

Chira, S. (March 5, 1994). Hilary Clinton seeks balance in news coverage of violence. *New York Times.*

Cleare, A. J., & Bond, A. J. (1994). Effects of alterations in plasma tryptophan levels on aggressive feelings. *Archives of General Psychiatry, 51,* 1004–1005.

Coccaro, E. F., et al. (1990). Fluoxetine treatment of impulsive aggression in DSM-IIIR personality disorder patients. *Journal of Clinical Psychopharmacology, 10,* 373–375.

Coccaro, E. F., et al. (1989). Serotonergic studies in patients with affective and personality disorders. *Archives of General Psychiatry, 46,* 587–599.

Colenda, C. (May 21, 1988). Buspirone in treatment of agitated demented patient. *Lancet,* p. 1169.

Comstock, G. A., & Strasburger, V. C. (1990). Deceptive appearances: Television violence and aggressive behavior. *Journal of Adolescent Health Care, 11,* 31–44.

Cornelius, J. R., et al. (1990). Fluoxetine trial in borderline personality disorder. *Psychopharmacology Bulletin, 26,* 151–154.

Corrigan, P. W., Yudofsky, S. C., & Silver, J. M. (1993). Pharmacological and behavioral treatments for aggressive psychiatric inpatients. *Hospitals and Community Psychiatry, 44,* 125–133.

Craig, T. J. (1982). An epidemiological study of problems associated with violence among psychiatric inpatients. *American Journal of Psychiatry, 139,* 1262–1266.

Cummings, J. L. (1985). Behavioral disorders associated with frontal lobe injury. In J. L. Cummings (Ed), *Clinical neuropsychiatry* (pp. 95–116). Orlando: Grune & Stratton.

Damasio, A. R., Tranel, D., & Damasio, H. (1990). Individuals with sociopathic behavior caused by frontal damage fail to respond autonomically to social stimuli. *Behavioral Brain Research, 41,* 81–94.

Dansk & Brewerton. (1994). *The National Women's Study.* Charleston, SC: Medical University of South Carolina, Crime Victims Research and Treatment Center.

Dateline NBC (October 28, 1997) telecast.

de Becker, G. (1997). *The gift of fear.* Boston: Little, Brown and Company.

De Koning, P., et al. (1991). Early clinical results in patients with aggressive behavior. In *Duphar aggression research: Preclinical and clinical data on eltoprazine*. Proceedings of the Fifth World Congress of Biological Psychiatry, Florence, Italy.

DeAngelis, T. (June 1995). Juror stress can influence final verdict. *APA Monitor*.

Delgado Escueta, A.V., et al. (1981). The nature of aggression during epileptic seizures. *New England Journal of Medicine, 305*, 696–698.

Deviney, E., Dickert, J., & Lockwood, R. (1983). The care of pets within child abusing families. *International Journal for the Study of Animal Problems, 4*, 321–329.

Devinsky, O., & Bear, D. (1984). Varieties of aggressive behavior in temporal lobe epilepsy. *American Journal of Psychiatry, 141*, 651–656.

Dietch, J. T., & Jennings, R. K. (1988). Aggressive dyscontrol in patients treated with benzodiazepines. *Journal of Clinical Psychiatry, 49*, 184–188.

Dobash, R. E., & Dobash, R. (1979). *Violence against wives*. New York: Free Press.

Dutton, D., & Painter, S. L. (1981). Traumatic bonding: The development of emotional attachments in battered women and other relationships of intermittent abuse. *Victimology: An International Journal, 6*, 139–155.

Dutton, M. A. (1992). *Empowering and healing the battered women*. New York: Springer.

Dutton, M. A., Hohnecker, L. C., Halle, P. M., & Burghardt, K. J. (1994). Traumatic responses among battered women who kill. *Journal of Traumatic Stress, 7*(4), 549–564.

Dwyer, J. (March 29, 1998). Kids trained to kill "people" who don't die. *Daily News*, p. 4.

Editorial: Ideas for our community: Stop the violent cycle: Understanding domestic abuse is essential to ending it. (October 13, 1997). *Atlanta Constitution*, p. A12.

Elphick, M. (1989). Clinical issues in the use of carbamazepines in psychiatry: A review. *Psychological Medicine, 19*, 591–604.

Elrod, L. D. (1995). Family law in the fifty states: 1993–1994. *Family Law Quarterly, 28*, 573–706.

Ewing, C. P. (1987). *Battered women who kill: Psychological self-defense as legal justification*. Lexington, MA: Lexington Books.

Fauman, B. J., & Fauman, M. A. (1982). Phencyclidine abuse and crime: A psychiatric perspective. *Bulletin of the American Academy of Psychiatry & Law, 10*, 171–176.

FDA Drug Bulletin. (1971). *Use of drugs for unapproved indications: Your legal responsibility.* Washington, DC: Food and Drug Administration.

Federal Bureau of Investigation. (1991). *Uniform crime report.* Washington, DC: Author.

Feldman, T. B., & Bell, R. A. (1993). Juror stress: Identification and intervention. *Bulletin of the American Academy of Psychiatry and the Law, 20*(4), 409–417.

Ferraro, K. (1993). Cops, courts, and women battering. In P. B. Bart & E. G. Moran (Eds.), *Violence against women: The bloody footprints* (pp. 165–176). Newbury Park, CA: Sage.

Finkelhor, D., Hotaling, G. T., & Yllo, K. (1988). *Stopping family violence: Research priorities for the coming decade.* Newbury Park, CA: Sage.

Finkelhor, D., & Yllo, K. (1985). *Licensed to rape: Sexual abuse of wives.* New York: Free Press.

Fishbein, D. H., Zovsky, D., & Jaffe, J. H. (1989). Impulsivity, aggression and heuroendocrine responses to serotonergic stimulation in substance abusers. *Biological Psychiatry, 25,* 1049–1066.

Florida Statutes Annotated sec. 61.13(b)(2) (West 1994).

Forster, P. L., Schoenfeld, F. B., Marmar, C. R., & Lang, A. J. (1995). Lithium for irritability and post traumatic stress disorder. *Journal of Traumatic Stress, 8*(1), 143–149.

Friedman, L., & Cooper, S. (1987). *The cost of domestic violence.* New York: Victim Services Research Department.

Furse, J. (May 16, 1995). A violent epidemic: Harrowing tales of domestic abuse. *Daily News,* p. 7.

Galvin, T. (April 24, 1997). Few battered women getting shelter. *Daily News,* p. 8.

Gannett News Service. (June 23, 1992). Widow blames stress of jury duty on husband's death. LEXIS news file.

Gelles, R. J., & Straus, M. A. (1988). *Intimate violence.* New York: Simon & Schuster.

Gerbner, G., Gross, L., Morgan, M., & Signorielli, N. (1980). The mainstreaming of America: Violence profile no. 11. *Journal of Communication, 30*(3), 10–29.

Glazer, S. (February 1993). Violence against women, *CQ Researcher, Congressional Quarterly, 3*(8), 171.

Glenn, M. B., et al. (1989). Lithium carbonate for aggressive behavior or affective instability in ten brain injured patients. *American Journal of Physical and Medical Rehabilitation, 68,* 221–226.

Goldberg, C. (November 11, 1997). In a startling turnabout, judge sets au pair free. *New York Times*, pp. A1, A22.

Goldstein, J., Freud, A., & Solnit, A. J. (1973). *Beyond the best interests of the child*. New York: Free Press.

Granville-Grossman, K., & Turner, P. (1966). The effect of propranolol on anxiety. *Lancet, 1,* 788–790.

Greendyke, R., et al. (1986). Propranolol in the treatment of assaultive patients with organic brain disease: A double-blind crossover, placebo controlled study. *Journal of Nervous and Mental Disorders, 5,* 290–294.

Greendyke, R., & Kanter, D. (1986). Therapeutic effects of pinodolol on behavioral disturbances associated with organic brain disease: A double blind study. *Journal of Clinical Psychiatry, 47,* 423–426.

Hafemeister, T. (1993). Juror stress. *Violence and Victims, 8*(2), 177–186.

Hafemeister, T., & Ventis, L. (1992). Juror stress: What burden have we placed on our juries? *State Court Journal, 16*(4), 35–46.

Hamilton, A. (September 29, 1997). Jurors say effects of trial still felt. *Dallas Morning News.*

Hampton, H., et al. (1993). *Family violence: Prevention and treatment.* Newbury Park, CA: Sage.

Haralambie, A. M. (1993). *Handling child custody, abuse, and adoption cases.* Colorado Springs: Shepard's/McGraw-Hill.

Hauser, J. (February 13–19, 1997). Jurors' rights are dealt a blow. *Boulder Weekly.*

Hilton, N. Z. (1992). Battered women's concerns about their children witnessing wife assault. *Journal of Interpersonal Violence, 7,* 77–86.

Hinshaw, S. P., Buhrmester, D., & Heller, T. (1989a). Anger control in response to verbal provocation: Effects of stimulant medication for boys with ADHD. *Journal of Abnormal Child Psychology, 17,* 393–407.

Hinshaw, S. P., et al. (1989b). Aggressive, prosocial, and nonsocial behavior in hyperactive boys: Dose effects of methylphenidate in naturalistic settings. *Journal of Consulting Clinical Psychology, 57,* 636–643.

Hoffman, J. (July 10, 1994). Defending men who kill their loved ones. *New York Times.*

Holcomb, W. R., & Anderson, W. P. (1983). Alcohol and multiple drug use in accused murderers. *Psychological Reports, 52,* 159–164.

Holtz, H., & Furniss, K. (1993). The health care provider's role in domestic violence. *Trends in Health Care, Law & Ethics, 8*(2), 47.

Howell, R. (September 26, 1993). UN: 90% of youth murder is in US. *Newsday,* p. 4.

Huesmann, L. R., & Moise, J. (June 1996). Media violence: A demonstrated public health threat to children. *Harvard Mental Health Newsletter.*

Huessy, H. R. (1992). Comorbidity of attention deficit hyperactivity disorder and other disorders. *American Journal of Psychiatry, 149,* 148.

Huston, A., Donnerstein, E., et al. (1992) *Big world, small screen.* Lincoln: University of Nebraska Press.

Itil, T. M., & Reisberg, B. (1978). Pharmacologic treatment of aggressive syndromes. *Current Psychiatric Therapies, 18,* 137–142.

Kaplan, S. L., et al. (1990). Effects of methylphenidate on adolescents with aggressive conduct disorder and ADHD: A preliminary report. *Journal of the American Academy of Child and Adolescent Psychiatry, 29,* 719–723.

Kaplan, S. M., & Winget, C. (1992). The occupational hazards of jury duty. *Bulletin of the American Academy of Psychiatry and the Law, 20*(3), 325–333.

Kardiner, L. (1941). *The traumatic neurosis of war.* New York: Harper & Row.

Kelley, J. E. (1994). Addressing juror stress: A trial judge's perspective. *Drake Law Review, 43*(1), 97–125.

Kelly, J. B., Zlatchin, C., & Shawn, J. (1985). Divorce mediation: Process, prospects, and professional issues. In C. P. Ewing (Ed.), *Psychology, psychiatry and the law: A clinical and forensic handbook* (pp. 243–280). Sarasota, FL: Professional Resource.

Kennedy, H. (October 12, 1997). Teens still out to kill. *Daily News,* p. 33.

Kennedy, H. (November 11, 1997). Juror: She deserved more time. *Daily News,* p. 28.

Kilpatrick, D. G., Edmunds, C. N., & Seymour, A. (1992). *Rape in America: A report to the nation.* Arlington, VA: National Victim Center.

Kirpatrick, B., Best, C. L., Veronen, L. J., Amick, E. A., Villeponteaux, L. A., & Rusk, D. A. (1985). Mental health correlates of criminal victimization: A random community survey. *Journal of Counseling and Criminal Psychology, 53,* 866–873.

Kleinman, S. B. (1990). Liberty and tardive dyskinesia: Informed consent to antipsychotic medication in the forensic psychiatric hospital. *Journal of Forensic Sciences, 35,* 1155–1162.

Koss, M. P., & Harvey, M. R. (1991). *The rape victim: Clinical and community interventions* (2nd ed.). Newbury Park, CA: Sage.

Kravtiz, H. M., & Fawcett, J. (1994). Serenics for aggressive behaviors. *Psychiatric Annals, 24,* 453–465.

Kruesi, M. J. P., et al. (1990). CSF monamine metabolites, aggression and impulsivity in disruptive behavior disorders of children and adolescents. *Archives of General Psychiatry, 47,* 419–426.

Lambiet, J., Marzulli, J., & Gentile, D. (October 12, 1996). Guns ex-wife, kills self, protection order found in his car. *Daily News,* p. 7.

Leicester, J. (1982). Temper tantrums, epilepsy, and episodic dyscontrol. *British Journal of Psychiatry, 141,* 262–266.

Lemert, J. B. (1989). *Criticizing the media: Empirical approaches.* Newbury Park, CA: Sage.

Levine, A. M. (1988). Buspirone and agitation in head injury. *Brain Injury, 2,* 165–167.

Levine, M., & Doueck, H. J. (1995). *The impact of mandated reporting on the therapeutic process: Picking up the pieces.* Thousand Oaks, CA: Sage.

Levy, B. (1991). *Dating violence: Young women in danger.* Seattle, WA: Seal.

Lewis v. Lewis, 637 A.2d 70 (D.C. 1994).

Libertarian Party of Boulder County. (October 1, 1996). Colorado judge threatens juror. *M2 PressWire.*

Mahoney, M. (1992). Legal images of battered women: Redefining the issue of separation. *Michigan Law Review, 90,* 1–94.

Malnic, E. (March 9, 1993). Forman in Simi Valley trial says riots, "national hate" stressed jury. *Los Angeles Times,* p. A18.

Marini, J. L., & Sheard, M. H. (1977). Anti-aggressive effects of lithium ion in man. *Acta Psychiatrica Scandinavica, 55,* 269–286.

Mattes, J. A. (1986). Psychopharmacology of temper outbursts: A review. *Journal of Nervous and Mental Disorders, 174,* 464–470.

Mauro, T. (October 3, 1995). Jurors are in for another trial: Getting their lives back. *USA Today.*

McQuillan, A., Lambiet, J., & Siemuszko, C. (February 14, 1996). Freed to kill: Judge released obsessed stalker. *Daily News,* p. 5.

Meyers, M. (October 1994). *Assigning blame: TV news, crime, and gender.* Paper presented at International Conference on Violence in the Media, New York, NY.

Meyers, M. (1994). News of battering. *Journal of Communication, 44*(2), 47–63.

Meyers, M. (1997). *News coverage of violence against women: Engendering blame.* Newbury Park, CA: Sage.

Michigan Comp. Laws. Annotated 722.23 (West 1994).

Missouri Annotated Statutes sec. 452.375 (Vernon Supp. 1994).

Money, J. (1970). Use of an androgen depleting hormone in the treatment of male sex offenders. *Journal of Sex Research, 6,* 165–172.

Monroe, R. R. (1985). Episodic behavioral disorders and limbic ictus. *Comprehensive Psychiatry, 26,* 466–479.

Morand, C., & Young, S. N. (1983). Clinical response of aggressive schizophrenics to oral tryptophan. *Biological Psychiatry, 18,* 575–578.

Morgan, R. (1994). *The word of a woman: Feminist dispatches.* New York: Norton.

Moyer, K. E. (1971). The physiology of aggression and the implications for aggression control. In J. L. Singer (Ed.), *The control of aggression and violence: Cognitive and physiology factors* (pp. 61–92). New York: Academic Press.

Nash, C. (July 26, 1994). $200 bail in rape riles prosecutor. *Newsday,* p. A21.

Nash C. (April 13, 1995). Cops: Woman blasted spouse with shotgun, Husband listed as critical after shooting. *Newsday,* p. A29.

National Television Violence Study. (1996). Mediascope. Studio City, CA.

National Victim Center. (February, 1993). *Helpful guide for victims of stalking.* New York: Author.

National Victim Center and the Crime Victims Research and Treatment Center. (April 23, 1992). *Rape in America: A report to the nation.* Charleston, SC: Author.

New York Victim Service Agency Report. (1987). *Costs of domestic violence.*

North Dakota Cent. Code sec. 14–09–06.2(j) (1993).

O'Dell, A. (October 1996). *Effective investigation: Tips on corroborating the circumstantial domestic violence case.* Lecture presented at the National Conference on Domestic Violence, Atlanta, GA.

Oklahoma Statutes Annotated title 43, sec. 112.2 (West 1990).

Olivier, B., et al. (1990). Serenics. *Drug News and Perspectives,* p. 3.

O'Shaughnessy, P. (October 12, 1997). Tragic cycle of victims. *Daily News.*

Pagelow, M. D. (1981). *Women battering: Victims and their experiences.* Beverly Hills, CA: Sage.

Pasternak, J. (September 8, 1997). Cat massacre at Iowa shelter splits town. *Los Angeles Times*, p. A1.

Pence, E., & Paymar, M. (1986). *Power and control: Tactics of men who batter*. Duluth, MN: Domestic Abuse Intervention Project.

Pullella, P. (January 24, 1996). Pope urges women to protest media exploitation. Reuters.

Ratey, J., et al. (1989). Buspirone therapy for maladaptive behavior and anxiety in developmentally disabled persons. *Journal of Clinical Psychiatry, 50*, 382–384.

Ratey, J. J., & Gordon, A. (1993). The psychopharmacology of aggression: Toward a new day. *Psychopharmacology Bulletin, 29*, 65–73.

Ratey, J., Gutheil C., & Leveroni, C. (1991). Clinical aggression research conference: Concluding remarks. *Journal of Neuropsychiatry, 3*, S69–S74.

Ratey, J., & Lindem, K. (1991). Beta-blockers as primary treatment for aggression and self-injury in the developmentally disabled. In J. Ratey (Ed.), *Mental retardation: Developing pharmacotherapies*. Washington, DC: American Psychiatry Press.

Ratey J., et al. (1993). The effects of clozapine on severely aggressive psychiatric inpatients on a difficult to manage unit of a state hospital. *Journal of Clinical Psychiatry, 54*, 1–6.

Ratey, J., Sands, S., & O'Driscoll, G. (1986). The phenomenology of recovery in a chronic schizophrenia. *Psychiatry, 49*, 277–289.

Ratey, J., Sorgi, P., & Polakoff, S. (1985). Nadolol as a treatment of akathisia. *American Journal of Psychiatry, 142*, 640–642.

Renzetti, C. M. (1992). *Violent betrayal: Partner abuse in lesbian relationships*. Newbury Park, CA: Sage.

Rickels, K., Freeman, E., & Sondheimer, S. (April 8, 1989). Buspirone in treatment of premenstrual syndrome. *Lancet*, p. 177.

Roan, S. (September 22, 1995). Under pressure, isolation: Jury stress sparks concerns. *Los Angeles Times*, p. A1.

Rohrlich, T. (April 23, 1993). Tempers flared, emotions ran high for King jury. *Los Angeles Times*, p. A1.

Roland, H. (October 1994). *Prospective on gender and rape myth acceptance: Challenging the sexual assumptions underlying music videos*. Paper presented at the International Conference on Violence in the Media, New York, NY.

Roper, Starch Worldwide Survey for Liz Claiborne. (July–August 1994).

Addressing domestic violence: A corporate response. New York: Liz Claiborne Inc.

Rosenfeld, M. (October 28, 1994). Mercy for a cuckolded killer: Women outraged over judge's light sentence. *Washington Post*, p. C1.

Schatzman, D. (May 24, 1995). Health of dismissed juror big concern. *Los Angeles Sentinel*, p. PG.

Schechter & Gray. (1988). A framework for understanding and empowering battered women. In M. Strauss (Ed.), *Abuse and victimization across the life span* (p. 242). Baltimore, MD: Johns Hopkins University Press.

Schornstein, S. (1997). *Domestic violence and healthcare: What every professional needs to know.* Thousand Oaks, CA: Sage.

Schwengels, M., & Lemert, J. B. (Spring, 1986). Fair warning: A comparison of police and newspaper reports of rape. *Newspaper Research Journal, 7,* 35–42.

Scott, E., & Derdeyn, A. (1984). Rethinking joint custody. *Ohio State Law Journal, 45,* 455–498.

Seligman, M. (1975). *Helplessness: On depression, development, and death.* San Francisco: Freeman.

Seligman, M., et al. (1968). Alleviation of learned helplessness in the dog. *Journal of Abnormal Psychology, 73,* 256–262.

Shay, J. O. (1992). Fluoxetine reduces explosiveness and elevates mood of Vietnam combat vets with PTSD. *Journal of Traumatic Stress, 5,* 97–101.

Shuman, D. W., Hamilton, J. A., & Daley, C. E. (1994). The health effects of jury service. *Law and Psychology Review, 18,* 267–307.

Smith, J. V. (September 19, 1997). Convicted juror files for appeal. *The Mountain Ear.*

Sobin, P., Schneider, L., & McDermott, H. (1989). Fluoxetine in the treatment of agitated dementia. *American Journal of Psychiatry, 146,* 12.

Sonkin, D. J., Martin, D., & Walker, L. E. (Eds.). (1985). *The male batterer: A treatment approach.* New York: Springer.

Soothill, K., & Walby, S. (1991). *Sex crime in the news.* London: Routledge.

Sparks, G. G. (October 1994). *Children's fright and anxiety responses to television and movies: The neglected effects of media violence.* Paper presented at the International Conference on Violence in the Media, New York, NY.

Stasi, L. (May 15, 1995). Who will help her? *Daily News,* p. 4.

Stout, K. D. (1991). Women who kill: Offenders or defenders? *Affilia, 6*(4): 8–22.

Straus, M. A., Gelles, R. J., & Steinmetz, S. K. (1980). *Behind closed doors: Violence in the American family.* Garden City, NY: Anchor/ Doubleday.

Sutton, L. (July 31, 1996). Suffolk hubby kills wife, self. *Daily News,* QLI p. 1.

Swanson, J. W., et al. (1990). Violence and psychiatric disorder in the community: Evidence from the epidemiologic catchment area surveys. *Hospital and Community Psychiatry, 41,* 761–770.

Tardiff, K. (1992). The current state of psychiatry in the treatment of violent patients. *Archives of General Psychiatry, 49,* 493–499.

Taylor, C. L. (October 9, 1992). Witness: I feigned sleep as dog ate baby. *New York Newsday,* p. 29.

Taylor, P. J., & Gunn, J. (1984). Violence and psychosis. *British Medical Journal, 288,* 1945–1949.

USA Today Survey. (May 10, 1994). *USA Today.*

U.S. Department of Justice. (1993). *Crime in the United States,1992.* Washington, DC: Author.

U.S. Department of Justice. (1994a). *Violence against women: A national crime victimization survey.* Washington, DC: Author.

U.S. Department of Justice. (1994b). *Violence between intimates.* Washington, DC: Author.

U.S. Department of Labor, Women's Bureau. (October, 1996). Domestic violence: A workplace issue. In *Facts on Working Women,* No. 96–3, citing *Fatal workplace injuries in 1994: A collection of data and analysis,* Report 908, Bureau of Labor Statistics, U.S. Department of Labor, July 1996. Washington, DC: Author.

U.S. Senate, Committee on the Judiciary. (October 1992). *Violence against women.* 102nd Congress of U.S. Senate, p. 3.

Valzelli, L. (1981). *Psychobiology of aggression and violence.* New York: Raven.

Valzelli, L. (1984). Reflections on experimental and human pathology of aggression. *Progress in Neuro-psychopharmacology & Biological Psychiatry, 8,* 311–325.

Valzelli, L. (1988). Notes on psychopharmacology of aggression. *Nordisk Psykiatrisk Tidsskrift, 42,* 465–470.

Van der Kolk, B. A. (1988). The trauma spectrum: The interaction of biological and social events in the genesis of the trauma response. *Journal of Traumatic Stress, 1*(3), 273–290.

Van der Kolk, B. A., & Greenberg, M. S. (1987). The psychobiology of the trauma response: Hyperarousal, constriction, and addiction to the traumatic response. In B. A. Van der Kolk (Ed.),

Psychological trauma (pp. 29–87). Washington, DC: American Psychiatric Press.

Van Praag, H. (1989). The role of serotonergic mechanism in aggression, auto aggression, and impulse control–indication. *Neurosciences and Behavior, 13*, 1.

Van Hasselt, V., Morrison, R., Bellack, A. S., & Hersen, M. *Handbook of family violence*. New York: Plenum.

Veltkamp, L. J., & Miller, T. (1990). Clinical strategies in recognizing spouse abuse. *Psychiatric Quarterly, 61*, 179–187.

Vermont Statutes Annotated title 15, sec. 655 (Supp. 1993).

Virginia Code Annotated sec. 20–124.3 (Michie Supp. 1994).

Walker, L. E. (1984). *The battered woman syndrome*. New York: Springer.

Walker, L. E. (1989). *Terrifying love: Why battered women kill and how society responds*. New York: Harper & Row.

Walker, L. E., & Edwall, G. E. (1987). Domestic violence and determination of custody and visitation. In D. J. Sonkin (Ed.), *Domestic violence on trial* (pp. 127–152). New York: Springer.

Ward, C. A. (1995). *Attitudes toward rape: Feminist and social psychological perspectives*. Thousand Oaks, CA: Sage.

Washington Post. (October 15, 1993). Denny beating trial judge releases juror transcripts, record reveals behavior before removing two and retaining one, p. A2.

Winslow, O. (May 31, 1996a). His deadly rage: Man kills wife who sought protection, hangs himself. *Newsday*, p. A3.

Winslow, O. (July 31, 1996b). "Say Hi to God": Making good on threats, man shoots wife, self to death. *Newsday*, p. A3.

Williams, D. T., Mehl, R., & Yudofsky, S. (1982). The effect of propranolol on uncontrolled rage outbursts in children and adolescents with organic brain dysfunction. *Journal of the American Academy of Child Psychiatry, 2*, 25–135.

Wishik, J., Bachman, D. L., & Beitsch, L. M. (1989). A neurobehavioral perspective of aggressive behavior: Implications for pharmacological management. In *Residential Treatment for Children & Youth* (Vol. 7, no. 2, 17–35). Binghamton, NY: Haworth.

Yesavage, J. A. (1983). Bipolar illness: Correlates of dangerous inpatient behavior. *British Journal of Psychiatry, 143*, 554–557.

Yudofsky, S., Silver, J., & Schneider, S. (1987). Pharmacologic treatment of aggression. *Psychiatric Annals, 17*, 397–407.

INDEX